SELL LIKE CRAZY

Sales Professional's Guide to Fame and Fortune

Phil Kreider

ISBN: 1451519192
ISBN-13: 9781451519198

"I sell, therefore I am. You buy, therefore I eat."

A s a sales *professional*, you are part of an elite society. There is a common bond all sales professionals share regardless of the product or service they sell or where they ply their trade. Membership in this *elite society* means you are entirely dependent upon your own abilities and entirely responsible for your own success—or failure. This makes a career in sales one of the most rewarding, challenging, exciting, and at times most *frightening* careers you can choose.

Professional selling is by no means a spectator sport. You must show up, suit up, and take the field if you want to play the game. *Winning* that game is what this book is all about.

I began my career in sales probably the same way many of you did—by accident. That "accident" has opened more doors of opportunity for me than I ever dreamed possible, and it has changed literally every aspect of my life for the better. I sincerely hope your career in sales has the same success and the same results in your life that it has had in mine. This was one of the main reasons I decided to write *SELL LIKE CRAZY*.

As for the skill and knowledge I acquired as a salesperson, much of it was a direct result of the assistance and guidance I received from others along the way. I was able to *learn* the art of selling because others took the time and effort to *teach* it to me. God bless all of them.

When I conduct my selling workshops and seminars around the country, there are often hundreds if not a few thousand audience members in attendance, all of them ready and able to become top sales professionals. The question is are they *willing*?

I begin each seminar by asking the attendees, "Who wants to make a million dollars this year?" At which point they all raise their hands. Then I admonish them for either not listening to my question or for lying. I then ask the same question again, "Who wants to make a million dollars this year? Once again, every hand in the room goes up. And once again, I tell them they either didn't understand the question or they're lying.

So I repeat the question one more time—who wants to make a million dollars this year? Only this time I add the following disclaimer:

"I asked a very specific question, 'Who wants to *make* a million dollars?' What I did not ask was who wants to *have* a million dollars. I already know the answer to that question. Of course, we all want to 'have' a million dollars; the homeless shelters and unemployment lines are full of people who want to 'have' a million dollars. But the question I asked was who wants to 'make' a million dollars?"

Merriam-Webster defines the word "make" as a *verb*, meaning to bring into being by forming, shaping, or altering; to cause to happen, exist, or be experienced by someone; to lay out and construct.

In my opinion, Webster's definition of the word "make" is the exact same definition that describes a successful career in selling. Read the definition of the word "make" again, and you'll see what I mean.

Welcome to the game of life. The exact same principles and strategies that are required for a successful career in sales are the exact same ones required for a successful life. If you can master the game of selling, you can master literally any aspect of your life.

There are very few places on earth outside of a sales office where you can learn, or be taught by trained professionals, all the principles of a successful life and how to create them for yourself. Review the chapter index of this book. You will see that every principle outlined for mastering a career in sales applies to mastering your life and environment.

Every sales industry, every sales organization, and every sales office has within it a group of individuals who know exactly what it takes to become a top sales professional. You will know who those individuals are because they themselves are top sales professionals. And the most important sale you can make is *yourself*, to those individuals in your sales environment who can show you exactly how to duplicate, if not exceed, their level of success. Why would they do that? Why should they care?

Because one of the first things top producers learn is that it is impossible to help someone else without helping yourself. How do you think those top producers first learned how to become top producers? Because someone probably took the time and effort to teach them how. You must become the instrument in which they repay that debt and pass on the good fortune they themselves have been dealt.

How do I know this? I have been a top producing salesperson most of my selling career. I have dealt directly with some of the top producing sales professionals in North America, and I can tell you that 99.9 percent of those individuals are not only ready, willing, and able to provide assistance, but are *eager* to do so. They just want to know that you value their time and effort as well as the wisdom they will share with you. But above all, they want you to *apply* it. Remember, when they take you under their wing, all the other birds in the tree are watching. What will they think of that top producer if the adopted fledgling crashes to earth when he leaves the nest? One of the most important attributes of top sales producers is their *reputation*. In this case, a host is only as good as its parasite.

If you do nothing more in your sales career than become the type of person that others want to see, if not directly help, become successful, then your success in this business is assured. If your peers want to see you succeed, then they will help and/or teach you how. If your customers want to see you succeed, they will buy and/or refer you to others. The ladder of success in sales is comprised of *people*. Some of those people you will sell to and some you will work with. Some you will be related to and know personally; one in particular you might even be married to. All of them will play a vital part in you becoming the sales professional and person that you always dreamed of becoming. You will only reach the top of the ladder on the shoulders of others. I think you already know that—that's probably why you're reading this book.

As I alluded to earlier, the three components of a successful sales career are ready, willing, and able.

Ready = Knowledge
Willing = Desire
Able = Skill

That's it—knowledge plus desire plus skill. Professional selling is an easy job...that's hard to do. For me, it was nothing more than the basics plus enthusiasm, repeated over and over again. I did what I was taught to do with as much excitement, optimism, and confidence as I could muster at the time. The plan worked—because I worked the plan.

You must not blow this opportunity. For whatever reason, life has delivered you to the right place at the right time to make all of your dreams come true—and maybe some other people's dreams as well. As a successful sales professional, you will have the ability to help people who will not receive that help unless it comes from you. You will be able to teach and mentor others who will never receive those things unless they come from you. Some of those people will be in those positions of need because they were not blessed to have a career of unlimited potential that literally taught them everything they needed to become successful. Life simply did not deal them that opportunity—but it did you. Don't blow it! Good hunting.

"I want you to start a crusade in your life—to dare to be your best."

WILLIAM DANFORTH

ACKNOWLEDGMENTS

"I would rather have a million friends than a million dollars." — EDWARD RICKENBACKER

'd like to thank all of those special people who helped me with my *life* in addition to my career and this book. Especially my Lord and Savior Jesus Christ.

My mother Sallie Patricia Dalia-Kreider—the only hero besides my wife Rachel I ever had. She raised me as a single mother until her passing in 1994, and provided me with everything I needed in life. She was a five-foot block of concrete straight out of Brooklyn, who never took an ounce of guff— ever. She was also the most caring, generous, and compassionate soul I ever encountered. God bless her.

My wife Rachel—my soul mate and the best friend I ever had. Her faith, strength, and love have kept me going through the many difficulties we have faced and overcome together through the years. I dare not even think of what I might have become without her by my side. Her loyalty, love, and wisdom are my most cherished possessions.

Acknowledgements

My lifelong pals from the *Flats* of Artesia, California—Robert Fort (Bob Ford the actor), Pete Degroot, Steve Goodwin, and Narcy Capote. What they say is true; you never have friends like the friends you make growing up.

My family. Especially my Uncles Philip and Vincent "Sonny" Dalia and my cousins Ramona and Ruthie. Growing up as an only child, I understand the value of a loving and supportive family. Even with them all the way across the country in my mom's native New York.

My other family. Annie, Scubby, Mama Girl, Tomato and Evander.

Matthew Chipman and Edwin Miller. Two great businessmen and business partners. And to our great company Evergreen Marketing, Inc. Home of TheGreenBaron.com.

Tom Swanner—the best damn real estate Broker in the business...and I should know. If you are a real estate professional in the Southern California area, Tom is the guy you want to work for—Century 21 Results, Inc.

A special thanks to Disneyland for still being "*The Happiest Place on Earth*" along with my adopted state of Maine; "*The Way Life Should Be.*"

Finally, I would like to thank the creators of the FOX television series *Fire Fly*. The best show in the history of TV. Too bad it was cancelled after only one season—but the good news is they made it a movie, *Serenity*.

> *"We are not human beings on a spiritual journey. We are spiritual beings on a human journey."*

ABOUT THE AUTHOR

$

Philip S. Kreider is chairman and CEO of Phil Kreider, LLC., a privately held company specializing in the acquisition and development of corporate, real and Internet related assets. Phil also serves as director or board member for several US based corporations and co-founded numerous companies and enterprises throughout North America.

Phil was born and raised in Artesia, California, graduating from Richard Gahr High School in 1978. Phil got his first taste of salesmanship as a newly licensed realtor in the early 1980s and has since gone on to author several books, training programs, and articles on the art of sales and business management. Phil is also a noted public speaker and is the founder of the sales training program and book by the same title, **SELL LIKE CRAZY**™.

Phil currently resides in central Maine with his wife, pop recording artist Rachel Jean.

For more information about Phil Kreider, please visit **www.PhilKreider.com**

SELL LIKE CRAZY!

Table of Contents

SELL LIKE CRAZY

The Salespersons Guide to Fame and Fortune

By

Phil Kreider

SECTION 1: Getting Ready

"Today's preparation determines tomorrow's achievements."

UNKNOWN

"Attitude is a little thing that makes a big difference"

UNKNOWN

"*I'll take attitude over ability any day,*" the company president told me when I asked why he had chosen *me* as the new vice-president. The promotion had come as quite a surprise, especially since I had been chosen over other candidates with obviously more experience, qualifications, and ability than myself. His explanation as to why he had chosen me was a lesson that would stay with me the rest of my life, and in no small way, shape my career in sales forever.

"One day you will have the experience and ability of the other candidates," he told me, "but they will *never* have your attitude." What a revelation! Never again would I let my lack of experience or knowledge become a barrier to my success. Regardless of the odds against me, my past failures, or the opinions of others, I would always be sure to arm myself with the *proper attitude* when beginning any challenge...and now I knew how important that "proper attitude" was.

Therein lies my challenge to you the reader—to commit right now, and for the remainder of this book, to develop and *maintain* a proper and positive mental attitude about yourself and your career. This will maximize the magnificent results I have planned for you in the following chapters and allow you to *go and grow* on your own far beyond the effects of this book.

Educational and growth opportunities are not destinations as much as they are *vehicles* that help you reach your destination; the key is to fuel and power such vehicles with the proper mental attitude to *reach* that destination. After all, if given the choice between running out of gas half way to your destination or not leaving at all, which would you choose? That is why attitude is so important—it's not only the difference between arriving at your destination or only getting halfway there, it's usually the difference between leaving for it in the first place.

What are you *really* selling?
Short answer: *Yourself*

Regardless of whatever products or services you may be currently offering to your customers, the first thing they need to buy is *you* before any sale is made—your products and services are secondary. If you can't make that first sale (you), then the customer probably won't have much interest in anything else you're peddling.

The first step is to sell *yourself* on you. Getting others to buy something that you do not believe in is akin to stealing in my opinion. There are too many valuable and needed products and services out there for any salesperson to waste his talent and time peddling *snake oil.*

A primary rule of professional salesmanship is that *it pays to be an optimist.*

1.   **Optimistic people try, do, and achieve more.**

2.   **An optimistic attitude fights depression, fear, and anxiety.**

3.   **Clients prefer and relate better to optimistic and up-beat salespeople.**

4.   **Optimism is contagious. (Unfortunately so is pessimism.)**

5.   **Optimistic people enjoy over-all better health and live longer.**

Here are a few basic characteristics shared by both optimistic and pessimistic types. Note which ones apply to you. In later chapters, you will learn specific techniques for developing and/or eliminating certain thought and behavior processes that may be hindering your performance; so take good notes now for future reference.

1.   **Optimistic people do not generally see failure and problems as long term. Rather, they see them as temporary setbacks that can and *will* eventually be overcome.**

2. **Pessimistic people usually view their problems and negative circumstances as entirely their own fault, as well being powerless to change them.**

3. **Pessimistic people tend to make decisions and take action based on a "worst case scenario," which, more often than not, leads to** *not* **making a decision or taking any action at all.**

4. **Optimistic people approach tasks with more of an** *ends* **mentality rather than a** *means* **one. A primary example of this would be in the area of client prospecting, generally viewed as a difficult or unpleasant necessity by most salespeople. The pessimistic personality would focus more on the "***means***" of the activity, such as the rejection, fear, and difficulty associated with prospecting—while the optimistic personality would be more focused on the** *end* **result of the activity, such as recognition, achievement, and money.**

Once you have achieved the first step of self-awareness, the next step is to begin *acting* on that awareness by beginning to make the necessary changes. I think you can see the obvious advantages to developing a positive mental attitude *prior* to starting any unpleasant or difficult activity, especially those necessary to your professional success.

Below I have listed a few initial steps you can begin taking right now to help create and establish a positive and more optimistic attitude as it relates to you and your career in sales. In order for these principles to take root and become *natural and habitual*, they must first be attempted on a limited yet constant basis. The more often these principles are applied (even in small steps at first), the more natural and habitual they will become over time.

1.   **Watch and control inner conversations: Did you notice I said watch "*and*" control? Awareness is worthless without action. We are all guilty of those subconscious and ongoing internal conversations we are constantly having with ourselves. I want you to pay especially close attention to those pre-programmed little *one-liners* that have become such a natural part of your inner conversations. So natural in fact, I bet many have become invisible to you often doing their damage completely unnoticed. You know the ones,** *"This will never work...I'm too this, or not enough that,"* **or whatever your personal mantras happen to be.**

As we will discuss later, those internal "one-liners" may have become so established and natural in your *subconscious*, as to be literally invisible to your *conscious* mind. The problem is they are *not* invisible. Your subconscious mind sees them loud and clear and reacts accordingly, or more accurately, it reacts as it has been allowed and trained to up till now. It hears every single internal conversation that you have with yourself. It not only *hears* those words, many times, it turns them into outward physical actions.

2.   **Learn to create balance: Find a balance between placing the blame where it belongs—by accepting**

personal responsibility for your choices and actions—and just beating yourself up mentally with no positive result at all other than discouragement and burnout. Don't get me wrong, a little mental reprimand is a good and necessary part of the change and growth process. Just practice *moderation*, and make sure whatever self-criticism you administer comes in the form of *constructive reinforcement*. Mistakes and setbacks often make the best learning experiences and opportunities for growth, as well as the necessary building blocks for future successes. I strongly encourage you to see those mistakes and setbacks for the golden opportunities for growth that they are, especially while you're right in the middle of them.

3. **Question negative thoughts: Stop them immediately! Or as I say,** *call their bluff.* **Try this technique the next time one of those negative thoughts hits you with something like, "Oh that's terrible." Immediately ask yourself the question "Is it really that terrible?"**

Getting hit by a bus crossing the street is *terrible*. Now, how does *your* "terrible" compare to getting hit by a bus? The next time your internal thought process tries to associate a negative attitude automatically with a particular situation or activity, such as prospecting for clients, or closing for the sale, *immediately* question that association. I believe that once you begin doing at least *that* initial step on a regular basis, you will soon be able to eliminate many of those self-defeating mindsets before they have a chance to take hold and begin affecting your actions.

4. **Have pre-established diversions: Have them in place and at the ready. If you are facing, or plan on facing, a situation where a negative or pessimistic frame of mind may hinder your performance, be prepared for it by having** *at the ready* **a pre-arranged activity, exercise, or distraction. This can help you gain the upper hand and fight off those negative thoughts.**

Some of those mental rituals, as I call them, have been going on for so long and repeated so often over the course of your life that they have become a habitual part of your natural physical actions. Automatically lighting up a cigarette during high-stress situations may be one of those. Some people, when faced with merely a *frustrating* situation, will reach for a cigarette *automatically*, and on such a natural, habitual, and subconscious level, they don't even realize they are doing it. (This is called conditioning).

For others it may be going for a walk (time-out) or having a cocktail. Whatever the ultimate manifestation, the reasons for them are basically the same—to divert your attention away from the unpleasant situation, instead of actually *toward* it and a successful resolution. The key is to develop positive and beneficial diversions that act as *performance enhancers* to replace those existing negative diversions that act more as *temporary pacifiers*.

5. **Accentuate the positive: Optimism pays. I cannot stress enough how vital a role a positive outlook and attitude**

will have on your performance as a sales professional. Unless you are excited enough about you, your product, or service, to sell the customer on that excitement, the customer can't get excited enough to buy. I know some of these exercises may seem silly at first, but compared to being broke, maybe silly isn't so bad.

Here are some common warning signs to look for if you feel you suffer from any pre-established pessimistic "triggers" or thinking processes.

6. Constantly seeking the approval of those around you

7. Not easily receptive to the viewpoints and opinions of others

8. Mistaking disapproval by others as disappointment in you as a person

9. Believing that if you disappoint others they will reject or abandon you

10. Thinking that your success as a person depends on what you achieve or earn

11. Mistaking temporary setbacks for permanent failures

12. Having a black or white, all or nothing outlook

13. Judging possible future outcomes by experiences of the past

14. Ignoring or trivializing your positive internal self-talk

15. **Assigning labels to situations instead of descriptions**

16. **Constantly second-guessing and doubting yourself and your capabilities**

17. **Over exaggeration of problems or negative situations**

18. **Constantly replaying negative experiences of the past in your mind's eye**

Do any of these sound familiar? Maybe even *very* familiar? Well, if they do exist, then at least now you're one step closer to understanding them, which actually brings you *several* steps closer to changing them. Awareness is the first step to change. It is also the first step toward any kind of education or self improvement. You can't fix what you don't even know is broken.

Before you can begin making dramatic improvements and changes on the *outside*, you must first begin to make them on the *inside*. The first step in the internal change process is to become aware of certain attitudes and mindsets that you have about yourself, your career, and your relationships within those circles. If you can first identify those inhibiting, destructive, and negative thought processes, then relate to them in a manageable way, you can then begin to remove and replace them altogether with empowering and positive thought patterns. This won't happen overnight, and it will take a *consistent* and *persistent* effort on your part.

Remember, those negative internal conversations aren't something that just happens to us. It's something *we talk ourselves into*. In other words, negativity is not a *noun*...it's a *verb*, which implies *action*. Again, negativity is not something that just happens to us; we have to *work* at it. So take some time off.

We have touched on only a few of the internal factors that affect and shape your attitudes and automatic thought processes. There are, of course, several external factors that take place, which can also shape and direct the way we see and react to certain situations. If we view something as being physically unpleasant, chances are we have already established negative mindsets and attitudes toward that unpleasant activity or situation. Many of those attitudes are so natural to our ongoing thought process they simply appear *automatically* whenever the unpleasant situation presents itself.

Unfortunately, most people never question the validity of those negative associations when they suddenly and automatically do appear. They simply view their arrival as normal and take for granted that their negative viewpoint is an accurate assessment of the situation. A good example of this would be the negative perception most people associate with rejection from others. In the field of sales, this would be the refusal by a potential customer to buy your product or service. *It happens.* In fact, the *more* it happens, the more money you make. If you are in the business of selling anything, then you are in the business of getting rejected. In other words, you get paid to hear the word "no." The key is to understand that not every response you get from a potential client is going to be a "no," and that those noes are nothing more than a step closer to a yes.

Most sales professions have statistical ratios that apply to the number of rejections received per sales made. Simply put, it's a numbers game. The words "yes" and "no" then become nothing more than "numbers." It might help to view a "yes" (sale) as the golden needle in the proverbial haystack of noes (rejection). One must sift through all the hay (rejection) in order to find the needle. Therefore, the more hay (noes) you statistically sift through, the more opportunities you have to find those needles (yeses).

The best way for any sales professional to approach rejection is to never, ever to take it personally. It is not *you* the person they are rejecting; it is the product or service you happen to be selling at the time. There are, of course, things that a sales professional can do to create a more lucrative sales environment in order to increase his hay to needle ratio. The key is to strike a balance between putting yourself in the position to be rejected, and detaching yourself as a person from it. Seeing both as mere "numbers" will help.

As a teacher and student of human development and performance enhancement, particularly as it relates to the field of professional sales, I have compiled a list of thirty-five characteristics shared by individuals who have excelled at their chosen professions.

1. **Maintain an** *attitude of gratitude*. **Count your blessings daily.**

2. **Life is difficult at times. Plan for and expect difficulties.**

3. **Prepare and condition yourself for prosperity.**

4. **Do your homework. Don't just learn the** "*tricks*" **of the trade.** *Learn the trade.*

5. **Know your strengths and how to use them.**

6. **Understand your weaknesses and how to overcome them.**

7. **Work hard** *and* **smart.**

8. **Focus on the positive.**

9. **Break down large objectives into bite-sized tasks.**

10. **Use notes to review and remember what you learn.**

11. **Take goals and dreams seriously.**

12. **Rehearse and plan for success.**

13. Understand that your destiny is by *choice* and not by chance.

14. Try to find at least one opportunity in every setback and failure.

15. Give yourself a pat on the back when deserved. (Carrot)

16. Give yourself a kick in the pants when deserved. (Stick)

17. Never say *never*.

18. Beware of the invisible killer—*procrastination*.

19. Learn to think like the *other guy* (customer, competitor, etc.).

20. Be self-reliant whenever possible. (If it is to be…it is up to *me*.)

21. Do not give into greed. It overrides internal defense mechanisms.

22. Have a mission in life and *write it down*.

23. Treat failure and success equally as the two impostors that they are.

24. Write down and keep everything positive or beneficial that you see, hear, or read.

25. **Choose your priorities carefully. To choose one road is to forsake another.**

26. **Do good for, and to, others whenever possible.**

27. **Keep your commitments. Finish what you start. (Number one cause of professional burnout)**

28. **Learn to forgive and forget. You'll live longer.**

29. **Try to be likable. It's the secret to selling** *anything.*

30. **Be fair to your adversaries. Today's opponent may be tomorrow's ally.**

31. **Beware the opinions of** *experts.*

32. **Get** *serious.*

33. **Get** *smart.*

34. **Get** *excited.*

35. **Get** *going.*

When I was a professional trainer for newly licensed realtors, I would always ask the class what their biggest fear was as a *newbie.* Easily, 90 percent of the class said it was the fear of being asked by a client how long they've been in the business, which for most of them could be counted in *days.* I then asked those respondents, "Why do you suppose they'll ask that question?"

You would not believe the nightmare scenarios some of them came up with. They gave answers ranging from, "They hate me," to, "They're looking for an excuse not to hire me."

Seldom did I ever hear the number one reason clients ask salespeople how long they've been in the business—they're just curious! So I gave them a stock answer to use when faced with that question, "Man, it seems like forever sometimes."

Years later, many of those same salespeople told me they used that very answer when posed that question by some of their clients...and none of the clients ever brought it up again. Like I said, they're just curious.

Before any of those new agents even got to meet their first potential client, they had already concocted every worst case scenario they could think of for a problem that only existed in their mind. Being "new" at something is not a problem, unless you "believe" it is...or isn't.

It was not so much a fear of the actual question, "How new are you?" It was their fear (lack of confidence) regarding how they would respond. When I gave them the magic phrase, so to speak, they were able to put those fears behind them, replace those fears with confidence and the proper mental attitude toward that perceived problem, then move on to the next thing they needed to learn. It was just that simple. Many of them knew they would face that very question, but now they did not fear or have lack of confidence in their ability to handle and overcome it.

The best thing you can do right now is to take some time and make a list of all the things you *believe* are hindering your career. Keep that list handy, because in later chapters we're going analyze those fears to determine their validity and the best plan of action for eliminating them. Then you can stop worrying about problems that may not even exist and get out there and *SELL LIKE CRAZY*!

"The real secret to success is enthusiasm."

WALTER CHRYSLER

CHAPTER 2: CONFIDENCE

"If you think you can win, you can win. Faith is necessary to victory." WILLIAM HAZLITT

*F*aith. I could write volumes on the subject. In fact, volumes *have* been written on the subject. I am not necessarily talking about the kind of faith it takes to move mountains. You would be amazed at how much just a little faith and belief can accomplish for you and your profession; the power of belief is *beyond* belief.

You must understand that faith is a *two-way* street. There is *negative* as well as *positive* faith. Negative faith is usually based on fear, doubt, or possibly a negative experience from the past. It usually manifests itself in the form of negative thoughts, beliefs, and statements long before the actual problem even arrives. Unfortunately, we act upon what we "believe" to be true more than we do on what the actual truth is.

How many times have you said something like, "I was afraid that was going to happen," or "I knew this wouldn't work out?" Those seemingly innocent little phrases are just the verbal manifestations of your internal thought process and belief system, often describing your *feelings* about the situation more so than the actual situation itself.

Positive faith goes back to what we discussed earlier. *It pays to be an optimist.* Optimistic thought patterns will display themselves in outward words and actions. The sooner you start *expecting* good things to happen, the sooner they *will* start to happen.

Another thing to avoid when it comes to developing and changing your own personal belief system is to not let *others* do it for you—for one simple reason, they do not know enough about you individually to have any degree of accuracy. When it comes to the subject of *you*, you are the expert.

If you have the desire, you can change your personal belief system. If you can change your beliefs, then you can change your world, and ultimately your destiny. You can consistently and effectively bring your dreams into reality by using very easy techniques to rein in those negative thought patterns that may have been hindering you so far, and begin replacing them with positive, self affirming beliefs. This will ultimately allow you to use those internal power sources to gain control of your external circumstances.

According to Dr. Walter Doyle Staples, these are the ten core beliefs that are unique to most peak performing men and women. I want you to consider each one carefully and imagine what your life would and could be like if you adopted these beliefs as your own.

1. **Winners are not born. They are** *made.*

2. **The dominant force in your existence is the way you think.**

3. **You can create your own reality.**

4. **There is some benefit to be had from every adversity.**

5. **Each one of your beliefs is a choice.**

6. **You are never defeated until you accept defeat as reality and stop trying.**

7. **The only real limitations on what you can accomplish are those you impose upon yourself.**

8. **You already posses the ability to excel in at least one key area in your life.**

9. **There can be no great success without great commitment.**

10. **You need the support and cooperation of other people to achieve any worthwhile goal.**

Would you knowingly engage in an activity that you knew was harmful to you? Perhaps even fatal? Of course not! Who would? And yet each day, millions reach for a cigarette in times of stress, boredom, or simply out of physical habit. Don't you think they are even partially aware of the dangers associated with cigarette smoking? Not just to themselves, but also, as studies have shown, to those around them as well? The dangers are clearly printed on the label! And yet, they still do it. Why? I believe it is because their belief system has linked more pleasure and advantages to destroying themselves, than it has to the perceived negatives of trying to stop such a powerful and destructive force in their lives. It is the exact same principle as your sales career. You already know things *not* to do, and yet you do them—often consistently. And you know the things you need to do, and yet hesitate in doing them or avoid them altogether. Each of which is probably nothing more than bad conditioning established over time until they became *habits*. Now it's time to break those habits by breaking the conditioning that established them in the first place. Kill the root and the weed dies.

The next step after removing those weeds is to replace them with something more positive—then nurture those new *seedlings* as well as the soil they are planted in (your mind). Fertile soil left unattended will only sprout more weeds. Removing the first batch of weeds is only the start. Gardening is a never-ending cycle.

What if you could change and/or recondition your attitudes and reactions to certain perceived negative situations to the point where you automatically viewed and responded to those same negative situations in a completely different manner? Not just "different," but in a more empowering and positive way (like replacing weeds with flowers)? What difference would that make to literally every situation and experience you faced? You could use just that one development to become the sales professional and person you always dreamed of becoming, in essence, changing your pre-existing negative beliefs into something that moved you closer to achieving your not-yet-existing positive beliefs.

You can, with a little effort, practice, and information, begin to change your actions simply by changing how you *feel* about those actions. Successful people are usually successful because they develop the habits of doing the things unsuccessful people don't like to do. Believe me; *they don't like to do them either*. The difference is they are able to control their actions by first controlling their attitudes regarding those actions—mind over matter.

The greatest tool in your arsenal when it comes to creating a positive mindset that views and reacts to negative situations in a more positive manner is *confidence*—the confidence that you are bigger than the problem you face, that you can handle the problem, and that regardless of the actual situation, you will react properly under the circumstances.

Your level of confidence should dictate your reaction to the situation, not vice-versa. Situations may not be able to be controlled to your level of satisfaction, but your reaction to them can be. You may not be satisfied with the situation or even the outcome, but you can always be satisfied with your attitude and reaction to those situations and outcomes. Sometimes that will be the only compensation you walk away with.

Most sales professionals probably understand the basic principle that increased *activity* leads to increased *productivity*. In other words, it's a numbers game. So why does an industry whose success is so easy to calculate still have one of the highest failure rates? Isn't it simply a matter of doing what we're supposed to in sufficient "numbers" to achieve our desired level of success? Then why is getting salespeople to do what they know and believe to be a necessary part of their survival so difficult? Short answer: lack of confidence—lack of confidence in themselves, their product or service, and at times even their very profession.

If you were absolutely confident that you were the best sales professional ever, you're more than half way to becoming the best salesperson ever, because a career in sales in 90 percent mental and 10 percent everything else. Therein lies the true secret of salesmanship; selling isn't so much a *numbers game* as it is a *mental* one. The salesperson that masters his/her own mind masters the game, not the other way around!

So what's the problem? Human beings are lazy by nature. If that were not the case, we never would have invented the wheel; we would still be dragging things around! The same is true for your pre-existing beliefs about yourself and your abilities (confidence). It's simply easier to drag them around all day than it is to change or fix those beliefs. It is also human nature to develop self-instilled fears and limitations long before we are actually confronted with them face to face (much like a fear of dying). That's why it is so important to almost *begin again* when it comes to our preconceived beliefs of what we *can* do, *should* do, and *will* do. From a mental standpoint, it may be necessary to hit the re-set button and begin again with the necessary level of confidence already *pre-established*. In other words, learn to be "confident" before you try to learn anything else. Stop worrying about worrying. Face even the most difficult and challenging situations with confidence...whether real or perceived.

There was a notable survey conducted identifying the number one fear among human beings. It was public speaking. The second biggest fear was death. That means at the average funeral, most of those in attendance would rather be in the casket than delivering the eulogy. In other words, most people would rather be dead than show a little confidence. If mourners were actually given that choice, it's a safe bet anyone with enough confidence to deliver the eulogy would probably be salesperson.

Confidence is nothing more than self-created optimism. And, as we discussed in the previous chapter, you must begin, just as the optimist does, to focus on the *ends* as opposed to the *means* in order to help create that confidence in the first place.

Let's go back to what I mentioned earlier. The difference between successful salespeople and unsuccessful salespeople is that the successful ones make a "habit" of doing the activities the unsuccessful ones hate doing. They don't just *do* them; they make a "habit" of doing them. Again...successful people don't like doing those activities any more than unsuccessful people do, but they do them anyway, and they do them regularly enough to develop them into habits. And therein lies the difference between success and failure in this business—habit. One group develops a habit of doing something and the other group develops a habit of *not* doing it. Both habits take effort and time to develop.

De-vel-op (*verb*): To cause to grow; to bring from latency to or toward fulfillment; to make visible or manifest.

So, what is the difference between those salespeople who "develop" the habits of doing the unpleasant activities that will make them successful and the ones who refuse to develop those habits? *Confidence*. Successful salespeople who overcome those unpleasant activities have more "confidence" in themselves to beat the problem than they have in the problem to beat them. Notice I didn't say more ability or experience (those things will come). I said "confidence." Ability and experience take time, but confidence can be created almost instantly...if you *believe*.

Con-fi-dence (*noun*): Assurance; freedom from doubt; belief in yourself and your abilities.

Have you accepted the fact that a career in sales often means repeating the same unpleasant activities continually for the duration of your career? The good news is that "fact" will eliminate 90 percent of your competitors before they even make their first few sales. Interesting concept—hating, avoiding, and fearing something that eliminates 90 percent of your competitors. No offense...but only a *salesperson* would think like that.

Mind over Matter
They say there is no reality—only *perceived* reality. In other words, what you *believe* to be true, is for you, even more true than the actual reality of the situation. To complicate *matters* (no pun intended) we often make up our own "reality" as we go. Improvising and adjusting along the way to handle and, hopefully, overcome certain difficult situations. The key is to have confidence in your ability to improvise and adjust to any situation effectively. If you first have the necessary confidence in yourself, regardless of the situation, then you will tend to believe (regardless of the situation) that you can overcome it...and for you, that becomes the new and improved reality.

Our level of self-confidence has a way of shaping our words and actions. Our words and actions ultimately determine who and what we become. As a result, we tend to become what we *think* about all day long. Control your thoughts and you ultimately control your *destiny*.

A more confident individual is able to "think" or focus on positive results (success) simply because he believes he is capable of achieving those successful results. We seldom think about things we don't think we can or ever will achieve—because those things are not "real" to us. Some might call that fantasy.

Fantasy (*noun*): Imagination unrestricted by reality.

Fantasy is exactly what we've been talking about—*unrestricting your reality*! And how do you do that? By unrestricting your confidence—let it run wild! For the next seven to fourteen days, pretend you can do *anything*. Pretend you are not afraid of any unpleasant activity associated with your professional performance. Pretend you have no limitations, that you are absolutely the best salesperson ever to work for your firm. Try acting and thinking like that for even a week and see how much it changes the rest of your career...and your life!

There is an old saying, "What the mind can conceive and believe, it can achieve." There is one example in particular often related to this concept. In ancient times, it was believed that the human body was physically incapable of running a mile in less than four minutes. This belief was even challenged by having hungry lions chase the runners to see, if under those extreme conditions, a mile could be run in less than four minutes. What they wound up with was no one that could do it, and several well fed lions. Then in 1954, a runner by the name of Roger Bannister finally broke the four-minute mile. The following year, several runners began breaking the four-minute mile. Consistently! No one could do it up to that point, and then suddenly, *everyone* was doing it. Today you must run a mile in less than four minutes to qualify for the high school track team.

What happened? Shorter miles? Super humans? Better track shoes? Slower lions?

None of the above. I believe it was because up until the point that it was actually done, people only *conceived* it. Once someone actually did it, he began to *believe* it. Then he began to *achieve* it.

I mentioned earlier not to let others determine your individual belief system. Others may be able to *predict* your future, but only *you*, can *determine it*—scary thought if you have more confidence in others than you do yourself.

What I would like you to do for the next week is to monitor your *self-talk*. Note everything you experience throughout the day, and your internal thoughts and conversations regarding each situation. Be sure to pay close attention to those pre-programmed messages we discussed earlier. I think that once the exercise is completed, and you have a chance to review your thoughts regarding the events of the day, you will be amazed at the level of negativity in which you have been viewing your circumstances. And that's just for a few days. Now multiply that over a lifetime of daily conditioning and you should get an idea of what needs to be done to create a new, optimistic, positive, and empowering mindset.

Once you have an awareness and understanding of the thought processes that have shaped your world up to this point, then you can begin to replace those negatives with positives. Once you have in place a basic positive mindset, then you can begin to exercise those thought patterns until they become as natural to you as the negative ones have been up to this point.

This metamorphosis is going to be a daily, as well as a lifelong, endeavor. The work of self improvement is never completed. The good news is after just a few weeks you should begin to notice dramatic changes. The difficult part of this process is always the first few steps. After that, the *new* way of thinking will begin to take root. Once the new way of thinking is in place, it will begin to manifest itself in new, more effective means of performance. Once you gain control of your actions, by first gaining control of your thoughts and beliefs, you can then gain control of your life, your career, and your future.

There is also another exercise I would like you to do. For the next few days, just before retiring, I want you to spend just a few minutes in a quiet uninterrupted place and imagine in your mind's eye, with as much detail as possible, what your life and your relationships would be like if you began achieving all of your career and financial goals.

You must begin to reinforce your desired results to your subconscious mind and not just the negative *what ifs* that have been dominating your thoughts so far. You must spend time every day creating a mental picture of exactly how you want your life to be. Find enough reasons *whys* and the *how tos* will come automatically.

> *"The only thing that stands between a man and what he wants from life is often merely the will to try it and the faith to believe that it is possible."*

> RICHARD M. DEVOS

CHAPTER 3: COMMITMENT

$

Consider a breakfast of bacon and eggs; the chicken may be *involved* in the breakfast, but the pig is *committed* to it.

Here is my definition of the word commitment.

1. For the duration; 2. Without contingencies; 3. No excuses!

Here are six effective strategies for strengthening and directing your level of commitment.

1. **Keep your commitments: The leading cause of career related stress and burnout is putting ourselves in situations where we fail to finish what we start. America represents roughly 10 percent of the world, yet we consume 90 percent of the world's tranquilizers. Our parents were right; don't make promises you can't keep and never bite off more than you can chew.**

2. **Put it in writing: Start with a simple list of goals—big and small, long term and short term, personal as well as**

professional. We'll cover this concept in greater detail during the goal setting section of this book.

3. **Create rewards and penalties:** Basically, the old carrot and stick. Rewards can be as grand as a summer vacation for you and the family or as simple as a morning cup of coffee. Penalties can be in the form of some sort of negative stimuli or even the denial of a reward. If this form of conditioning can work on lab rats, it can work on salespeople. Once your mind begins to link reward and pleasure, regardless of how small or simple, to certain desired activities, it will begin on a subconscious level as well as a conscious one to seek out those opportunities for reward, just as you will try to avoid opportunities for negative or punitive stimuli.

4. **Divide and Conquer:** It may pay to chop down your forests one tree at a time. Sometimes trying to view the big picture all at once can make a task or objective seem overwhelming or beyond our immediate capability. With that mindset, we may not even begin the task in the first place. Rather than viewing some tasks in their entirety, try to break them down into more manageable sub-tasks, then complete each one individually toward the completion of the whole.

5. **Set time frames:** It is important to establish specific time frames for the completion of certain tasks. This will give structured boundaries to operate within and ensure that you are on schedule and on track, as well as utilizing effective time management. Work has a way of expanding to the time allotted for its completion.

6. **Go public with it: Nothing creates commitment to a project than** *calling your shot.* **Sometimes putting your reputation on the line will provide that little extra incentive to keep you going and complete the task. Quitting is less an option when the eyes of the world are upon us. It also tells others around us what we are expecting from ourselves in the hope that they will expect it too. We often try harder to live up to the expectations others have for us than we try to achieve our own expectations for ourselves.**

The level of commitment I expected from my management and sales staff is simple—*onboard or overboard.* It doesn't matter to me so much what they commit to; more importantly, it is that they *keep* that commitment. Be careful what you promise—someone may actually expect you to do it!

Let's start with your current situation. What tasks or responsibilities have you been putting off that you know need to be done? That is the best place to begin with an exercise in commitment. Start by making a list of at least three activities you need to do *right now,* but haven't. Prioritize those activities and set reasonable time frames for their completion. It does not matter what the specific activities are; this is simply an exercise in setting commitments then keeping those commitments in an effective and timely manner.

Commitment is borne of desire. You must *want* to succeed and *want* to improve if the necessary growth and changes are to take place. The next step is of course to *act* on that commitment.

"Diamonds are nothing more than chunks of coal that stuck to their jobs."

MALCOLM STEVENSON FORBES

CHAPTER 4: OVERCOMING FEAR

I've heard it said that fear is an acronym for **F**alse **E**vidence **A**ppearing **R**eal. If true, then fear is a *lie*.

Imagine yourself in a high-pressure situation. Suddenly your senses come alive—the adrenaline starts pumping and you experience a heightened awareness of your surroundings and situation. Your hearing and visual senses are operating at maximum level; your thought process and reaction time is exponentially accelerated.

So what's happening here? What *external* trigger activated those enhanced reactions and performance? Here's a clue—it wasn't "external" at all. That "trigger" was internal...lying just under the surface inside of you. We call it fear.

The reason I would classify fear as an "internal" trigger is that some of us are afraid of things that others are not afraid of, and may even, in fact, enjoy. Therefore, we decide "internally" what we are afraid of externally. That means fear is a *choice*. Keep in mind I'm talking about the fears we face as professionals in this industry...not so much life or death scenarios. We'll call the career fears "little fears" that, as we've learned in the previous chapters, can successfully be overcome and even replaced with more positive and empowering beliefs.

In almost any situation, social or professional, where interaction with others exists, there is going to be some level of hesitancy, tension, or at least awkwardness—however slight. It may be in the form of intimidation by a superior or person in a position of authority over you, or maybe the very real fear of embarrassment while interacting with clients. Your fears regarding each of those scenarios is first established by your perception of that activity long before you actuality encounter it. Your mind simply looks ahead and sees what's coming, then makes some kind of judgment about it based on the limited information, experience, and resources available at the time.

Keep in mind, we often are more afraid of what we *don't* know than we are of what we do know—*fear of the unknown*. Therefore, the more you "know" the less you have to fear. Education and experience then become your biggest weapons against that which you currently fear. Notice that both education and experience are "mental" assets. Just like confidence, attitude, and commitment.

I've had very personable and relaxed relationships with several of my managers and supervisors over the years—the same superiors that many of the other staff members were so intimidated by they could barely bring themselves to look them in the eye.

Have you ever felt uncomfortable or been intimidated by certain individuals? We all have. I'll let you in on a little secret; it wasn't *them* you were afraid of—it was you. It wasn't how you felt about them; it was how you felt about yourself when you were around those individuals. We tend to see ourselves how we perceive *others* see us, whether that "perception" is real or not. If you have a negative attitude or opinion regarding a certain individual, it's probably based more on what you think they think of you, than what you really think of them. We tend to see others more as mirrors than as windows.

When a salesperson is more afraid of himself than the client, something's wrong.

For example, fear of embarrassment is the number one fear reported by sales professionals. Most in management agree this is the primary cause for failure within the industry.

I don't know if you will be able to conquer all of your fears relating to your career, but I do know that you can learn to operate successfully in spite of them. And for most top selling professionals, that's enough.

Fear can exhibit itself in many ways—some obvious, some not so obvious. One hidden, not so obvious way people exhibit their fears is to do just that—*hide* them. They may do this in a variety of ways, but the most common is called *compensating behavior patterns*. Simply put, using smoke to hide the fire.

I've seen some salespeople spend more time creating excuses for not doing certain activities than they would have spent actually doing those activities in the first place. I would often tell them that if they were as creative and dedicated to *doing* the work as they were at avoiding it, they'd be *my* boss right now and not vice-versa.

You'd be surprised at ways we avoid *and justify* the things we fear. Perhaps you recognize a few of these behavior patterns I've listed below—none being *too* familiar I hope.

1. **The getting ready to get ready syndrome: These are the people you see sitting at their desk while they are supposed to be prospecting or selling. Instead, they need to "get ready" first. The whole time probably thinking to themselves, "If I can just stay busy doing *this* stuff, I won't have to talk to any clients today." They won't even begin an activity until they have every tool, resource, fact, and so on, at their disposal. When they *do* get everything ready, they'll just find something else they can't do without.**

2. **The Super Genius: I have had a few of these in just about every sales office I ever worked in. They rationalize that**

if they can just create the *image* of success and knowledge, they could get away with *talking the talk* **without
having to** *walk the walk.*

3. The Analyzer: They could best be described as Super
    Geniuses trapped in the getting ready to get ready syn-
    drome. Without the latest technology, sales tools, train-
    ing, and anything else they can think of, they are un-
    able even to *begin* to do their job. And when they fail
    and have to leave the business, of course, it's always
    because the voicemail system was inadequate or the
    copier only printed in four colors instead of five.

4. The "I'm above that sort of thing" complex: These people
    equate salesmanship to peddling, and prospecting as
    beneath them. They rationalize their poor performance
    as not wanting to be one of those *pushy salespeople.*
    Their attitude is usually one of, "I only want to work with
    people who want to work with me." (Fear of rejection)

5. The Short-cutter: These are the people who outwardly
    display all the trappings of success. They invest heav-
    ily in the *appearance* of success rather than the tools
    and resources needed to attain it, usually to compen-
    sate for a low self image or lack of confidence. They
    usually display their success as a defense to their *ad-
    vertised* prosperity as opposed to their *actual* level.
    Much like most of us, they want success without the
    work or the risk. Unfortunately, they often feel that suc-
    cess is *owed* to them. They rationalize that they are
    more deserving of success because of who they are
    or the image they present, as opposed to what they
    actually do to earn it.

6. **The Apologetic: This is the salesperson with an almost "I'm sorry to have to do this" attitude when prospecting or closing for the sale. I see no other cause for this other than the fact that he either does not believe in himself, his product or service, or his profession. He rationalizes this reluctance based on** *it's a bad time, they're probably too busy*, **and so on. This type of personality also rationalizes that if he just acts nice or non- threatening enough, somehow the client will ask** *him* **for the sale. The sheep knows what the wolf is after. Believe me; you aren't fooling anyone. The client knows why you're there, and he knows what you want.**

There are several common fears related to a career in sales. I touched on a few of them earlier. Now I want to give you a more in-depth analogy of each, and possible ways for you to eliminate these negative associations and thought patterns. Of course, each individual is different, but I believe that just becoming aware that these mind sets exist within you is the first, and a very important, step in changing the way you view yourself and your career related duties.

1. **Understand that fear, more specifically overcoming it, is a necessary part of your success training and growth development. As I said earlier, awareness is the first step to change, education, and improvement. In other words, you can't fix what you don't know is broken.**

2. **Realize that many of your fears are usually an over exaggeration of the situation. Some people worry about everything, real or imagined. I on the other hand take the**

opposing view; don't tell me that worrying doesn't help. Because everything I worry about *never happens***!**

3. **Understand that at times fear can be a good thing. I began this chapter with the example of how your fears can heighten your senses and awareness in times or situations where it is necessary to operate mentally and physically at a higher level. Fear, in and of itself, is simply an internal defense mechanism. It is when those internal forces begin to affect your outward actions in a negative manner that you must take control of the fear, keep it in perspective, use it to your advantage, and learn to function despite it.**

4. **Make a decision that you are going to perform the task, despite the fears you have associated with it. Once you de-cide on almost anything, I think you'll find that your success in that endeavor is almost assured. The key is at least to** *be-gin* **the process, and that beginning starts with your deci-sion to do so. If that doesn't work, you can always go back to your old way of thinking and giving in to you fears.**

5. **Establish and commit to goals that push you beyond your comfort zone to a level of action you may have been afraid to try before. Set up a series of rewards and penalties as discussed earlier. Monitor your progress and keep track of how your fears and presumptions are affecting your performance. When you hit road blocks or setbacks, don't give up! Fear passes—results remain.**

Another very real, albeit contradictory fear that exists in almost every business endeavor is the fear of suc-cess. How can someone be afraid of succeeding you may ask? But think about it for a moment. With success comes responsibility and with responsibility comes pressure, commitments, and expectations by others. For some, the pressure of succeeding is greater than that of failing. Therein lies the challenge to anyone looking to rise above their current circumstances and overcome the obstacles that hinder their success—to accept the challenge of expecting more from themselves than anyone else possibly could.

Fear of success and the responsibility and changes that it brings can be as subtle as a gas leak—invisible but deadly. Below are some techniques you can use to help create the proper mindset.

1. **You must first convince** *yourself* **that you deserve success before you can convince others you deserve it.**

2. **You must begin to identify all the factors that currently exist in your life that are sabotaging and hindering your success. Once you create an awareness of those factors, you will discover that a majority of them are imagined or overblown to some extent, which goes back to what we discussed earlier.** *You* **are responsible for your actions and the outcomes they provide, as well as your reaction to those outcomes. Once you identify those inhibiting factors and mindsets, then you can begin replacing them with positive factors, attitudes, and actions.**

3. **Develop a written mission statement detailing exactly what you hope to accomplish on a professional level and a concise written plan of action for its attainment.**

We will discuss specific techniques for setting and achieving your goals in later chapters, but first we must begin to identify any negative mindsets that exist which may be hindering, or even preventing, you from giving it 100 percent when it comes to pursuing your dreams and a successful career in sales. The following is a test to see if you have any negative or uncomfortable associations related to succeeding.

1. **Do you feel uncomfortable accepting praise?**

2. **Do you downplay or ignore compliments?**

3. **Is your income within 10 percent of your parents and circle of friends?**

4. **Do you fail to follow up with opportunities for business?**

5. **Do you find that when you achieve goals it is not as satisfying as you thought it would be?**

6. **Do you do better at the start of a project then at the end?**

If you answered *yes* to any of these questions, then you may have an underlying fear of accomplishing more then you currently are. Fear of success begins with your established belief system. Those beliefs proceed to negative thinking, then to negative talk, then to negative actions, which ultimately leads to negative results. Your fears may create a pre-determined conclusion before you even started.

The problem with our fears is that we developed them long ago when we knew less about life than we know now. Humans are only born with two natural fears—falling and loud noises. Every other fear you developed over the course of your life and career you had to take the time and effort to *learn*.

The most effective way to overcome fear is by doing that which you fear and doing it until you are comfortable enough with it as not to avoid it. And that means leaving your comfort zone. Whatever fears you currently have do not reside in your "comfort zone." If they did, you wouldn't be afraid of them. That leaves two choices for a successful salesperson; learn to control your thoughts and actions to the point you can eliminate the fears altogether or learn to succeed in spite of them.

"Do what you fear most and you control fear."

Tom Hopkins

CHAPTER 5: DEALING WITH DISAPPOINTMENT

"No one that has ever lived has had enough power, prestige or knowledge to overcome the basic condition of all life—You win some. You lose some."

KEN KEYES, JR.

Sir Winston Churchill

Churchill's father considered his son so "dull" that he doubted whether he could ever earn a living. Churchill failed the entrance exam to Sandhurst twice! And was taken out of Harrow so that he could study with a tutor to avoid being expelled for low grades.

Thomas Edison

Edison's teachers described him as "addled." His father thought he was a "dunce." His teachers were constantly warning him that, "He would never make a success of anything."

Albert Einstein

Einstein stuttered until he was nine and spoke slowly after that. His poor performance in all of his classes prompted a teacher to ask him to drop out of school, telling him he would never amount to anything. Einstein failed his first two entrance exams at Zurich's Polytechnic Institute.

Sir Isaac Newton

Newton was allowed to get an education only because he proved to be a complete failure at running his family's business. In his first year, he finished dead last in his class.

Abraham Lincoln

1832: Fired from job; 1832: Defeated for legislature; 1833: Went bankrupt in private business; 1834: Elected to legislature; 1835: Childhood sweetheart dies; 1836: Suffers a nervous breakdown; 1836: Defeated for house speaker; 1843: Defeated for nomination to Congress; 1846: Elected to congress; 1848: Lost re-nomination to congress; 1849: Ran for land officer and lost; 1854: Defeated for senate; 1856: Defeated for nomination as vice-president; 1858: Defeated for senate, again; 1860: Elected president of the United States.

It's not the setbacks and failures we encounter in our lives that determine our futures. It is how we choose to react to, and overcome, them that ultimately decides their impact on us.

If you are in the business of sales, then you are in the business of *rejection*, and many times, *failure*. (Now you know what to say when someone asks what you do for a living.) If you have a problem handling that rejection and disappointment, there are only three things you can do at this point: close every sale, get out of the business, or successfully learn to *deal with disappointment*.

Disappointment, rejection, and failure are all contributing factors to job related stress and burnout, especially among salespeople. It's those very factors that give a career in sales one of the highest failure and attrition rates of any industry.

It is seldom the actual situation itself, as much as it is your *reaction* to it. Many of history's most noted figures where known less for their failures than they were for their triumphs over those failures. What history has also proven is great failures often create great opportunities, sometimes an opportunity for even a *failure* to make history.

When you think back over the course of your life, can you recall some tragedy or serious setback you experienced and thought to yourself at the time that you would never get over it—only to discover later that you *did* indeed get through it? Some of those incidents you may even be able to look back at now and laugh. In my personal experience, the major positive and beneficial turning points in my life usually resulted from some of my biggest failures and setbacks. Many, at the time, I was certain I would never recover from, let alone turn them into a future victory.

If you properly and enthusiastically apply the principles of this book, the good news is you should soon begin noticing positive changes occurring in the way you view, and react to, certain negative situations. The bad news is, along with those changes may come a certain amount of discomfort and fear, because change always means moving from our established comfort zone to a new and perhaps completely unfamiliar way of thinking and behaving.

Here are the four phases of stress and tension to watch for when implementing major changes in our life:

1. **Alarm**

2. **Resistance**

3. **Adaptation**

4. **Fatigue**

If you have ever been in a stressful situation, even for a short while, then you understand that this purely *mental* emotion has plenty of *physical* side effects. The worst, of course, being premature death (stress is the number one killer). When you are under stressful circumstances, even the slightest problem can be a major catastrophe when added to the already weighty burden of existing stress and anxiety. I know the rule of thumb is to leave your personal problems at home and your professional ones at the office. If you can do that then you have separated yourself from literally every salesperson I ever knew. The key is to strike a balance between the two, not letting one overwhelm or affect, to any great extent, the other.

Our professional problems *are* our personal problems. Something you spend one third of your life doing that provides everything for the survival of you and your loved ones is never merely a *job*.

Divide and Conquer. With a little *dividing and conquering*, you can minimize the effect some problems in your personal life have on your professional life, and vice-versa. The best technique is to "divide" or separate your problems from the rest of your life/career, then conquer them one at a time, one step at a time, until they're either manageable or removed altogether.

Your attempts to conquer those problems can be just as stressful as the actual problems themselves. Ignoring the problem does not remove the stress of trying to conquer it. Ignoring it usually only creates new problems and prolongs the impact of the original problem—which is why ostriches don't make good salespeople.

Here's a little *stress test* to see if your negative situations may be getting the best of you.

1. **Do you finish other's sentences before they do?**

2. **Do have an animated speech style, speaking excitedly with hand gestures, etc.?**

3. **Do you talk, walk, and eat quickly?**

4. **Do you become upset in slow lines or in traffic?**

5. Are you generally impatient when at work?

6. Are you disinterested in, or unaware of, small details?

7. Do you often over extend yourself by doing too many things at once?

8. Do you feel guilty when you relax or take time off?

9. Do you tend to link your self-worth to things or income?

10. Do you find yourself trying to schedule more and more activities into less and less time?

11. Do have an obsessive attention to time?

12. Do you exhibit nervous gestures, such as drumming fingers, tapping a pen, nail biting, etc.?

13. Do you consider yourself a *workaholic?*

14. Do you work hurriedly even without deadlines?

15. Do feel that you experience higher levels of anxiety or depression compared to others?

16. Do you rarely accept advice from others?

17. Do you reject self-help information?

18. Do you consider non-productive leisure time a waste of time?

19. Do you have a general mistrust of others?

20. Do you possess a need to say, "I told you so?"

If you answered "*yes*" to five or more of these questions, you may be experiencing a higher level of stress and anxiety than normal or necessary. Don't kid yourself. It *is* something you're going to have to deal with sooner or later. You better, since 70 percent of all major medical problems are *stress related.*

Here are two effective techniques you can use to help yourself deal better with the everyday stress and pressure of pursuing a career in sales.

Relaxation Technique
Find a comfortable and quiet place to be alone where you won't be interrupted. Get in a relaxed and comfortable position, preferably lying down with your eyes closed. Starting at your feet and working your way up your body, begin to tense and relax your muscles one at a time. Do this approximately ten times for each muscle. While you are doing the contract and relax method with your muscles, begin to take deep, calculated breaths—taking them slower and slower, deeper and deeper. I then want you to imagine yourself in the most relaxed setting you can think of—perhaps it's a quiet beach or a walk in the woods. I want you to see that image in your mind's eye as clearly and in as much detail as you can. Try to imagine how it might smell, or how it might sound,

or perhaps feel the warmth of the sun on your face. Make it as *real* to your subconscious mind as you possibly can. You may even wish to play an audio recording of the setting to help your imagination. Do whatever you can to re-create the relaxed setting in your mind.

Anticipation Technique

The next time you anticipate being in a pressure or tense situation, try to be as prepared as possible to deal with the upcoming circumstances. Get a good night's sleep or be as rested as possible. Utilize positive self-talk and internal dialogue. Use visualization to see yourself *already* in possession of the desired results. Mentally role-play and rehearse your anticipated objective. If possible, plan a positive activity for immediately after the scheduled event. On the other hand, I don't want you to *over* anticipate any problems either. Keep expectations low and energy levels high. Don't plan *on* problems as much as planning *for* them.

"We are all failures...at least the best of us are."

SIR JAMES M. BARRIE

SECTION 2: Getting Started

"I only hope we never lose sight of one thing... that it all started with a little mouse!"

WALT DISNEY

CHAPTER 6: GOAL SETTING

"If you don't know where you're going, how do you expect to get there?"   Basil S. Walsh

I f you're on the road to success...you'll need a map.

Before you begin creating your road map to success, you must first determine exactly where you are now, where you ultimately want to end up and the most expedient method of getting there. Your "map" will be your written plan of action for accomplishing the trip.

From this moment on, I want you to start taking every dream, goal, and desire that you have regarding every major aspect of your life as seriously *mentally* as you do the things in your life that are *physically* present. You must begin to see with as much detail as possible yourself *already in possession* "physically" of those things you currently desire mentally.

Goals and dreams are *things—physical things!* Those "things" are the reason we get out of bed in the morning, and they can keep us going even through the most difficult of times. From the moment we wake to the moment we retire, we are moving toward the completion of some goal or objective.

How can a dream come true without having that dream in the first place?

Choose your goals carefully. Remember the old adage, "Be careful what you wish for— you just may get it!" A good friend of mine wished for a new Corvette for as long as I've known him. Three years ago, he finally went ahead and bought one right off the showroom floor. A year later, he traded it in due to the high insurance premiums (and three speeding tickets). I told him the next time he wishes for something...wish for a way to pay for it too.

When it comes to choosing and pursuing our desires, I am reminded of what my mom used to tell me, "You may not be able to become *everything* you want in life, but you can become *anything* you want." If you've stuck with the book this, far I'm going to assume that one of things you want to become in life is a successful sales professional. So let's get started.

This is going to be a *working* chapter. In it, you will be given your first few assignments to *complete*. The key word here is "complete." In my book, if you didn't do it *right*, you didn't do it, *period*! So do it right, and do it right the *first* time; you may not have the time to go back and fix it later.

Purpose (*noun*): An anticipated outcome that is intended or that guides your planned actions.

Goals are a destination; purpose is the journey. Goals are chosen; purpose is discovered. Goals are outward manifestations; purpose is internal. Goals change, purpose doesn't.

> *"Would you tell me, please, which way I ought to go from here?"*
> *"That depends a good deal on where you are going," said the cat.*
> *"I don't much care where..." said Alice*
> *"Then it doesn't matter which way you go," said the cat.*
>
> LEWIS CARROLL
> (ALICE'S ADVENTURES IN WONDERLAND)

When it comes to setting and achieving your goals, keep the following principles in mind.

1. **Keep an open mind.**

2. **Take a common sense approach to everything.**

3. **Get on board mentally.**

4. **Develop a** *written* **plan of action.**

5. *Commit* **to the plan of action.**

6. *Work* **the plan of action.**

7. **Realize that goals change, purposes do not.**

8. **Remove the road blocks, not the dreams.**

9. **You can have anything, but not everything.**

10. *Inspect* **what you** *expect.*

11. **Control your thoughts.**

12. **Have faith in what you know and do.**

13. **Be consistent.**

14. **Be persistent.**

15. *Just do it!*

Any goal-setting program must include an accurate assessment of where you are now. Which leads us to the first exercise of the chapter: The Self Evaluation...and be honest!

Step 1: Make a list of at least ten major goals you would like to accomplish during your life.

Step 2: Make a list of factors you believe are keeping you from achieving those goals.

Step 3: Create a list of everything you can think of that you can begin doing *right now* to start eliminating those factors.

Step 4: Write a paragraph describing how you will feel in twelve months if you achieve those goals

Step 5: Write a description of yourself personally and professionally as if you had already achieved those goals. What would you be like? Where would you live? Etc.

Step 6: Write a paragraph describing what accomplishments you are most proud of and why.

The main purpose of this exercise is to develop an accurate and clear picture of where you currently are in life, and maybe how you got there. The objective is to provide a visual (written) overall picture of your current circumstances, any dissatisfactions you may have with them, and what factors you believe exist that are preventing you from changing your current circumstances into what you want them to be.

The real key is to see yourself *beyond* your current circumstances to where you want to be, instead of focusing on where you are now. The next step is to create an effective plan for the attainment of those future circumstances. Here are some effective strategies for achieving your goals.

1. **Get up early on a regular basis.**

2. **Adhere to a daily work schedule.**

3. **Read your goal statement aloud twice daily.**

4. **Listen to your affirmation tape once daily (explained later in this chapter).**

5. **Program yourself for success.**

6. **Model your mentor(s).**

7. **Do your visualization exercises daily.**

8. **Use a daily planner system to stay focused.**

9. **Take pride in your efforts and accomplishments.**

Your plan of action to accomplish your goals will include breaking down each goal into individual doable tasks that move you toward each goal's attainment. Each journey involves the first step as well as each subsequent step along the way.

Something very important to keep in mind when creating the individual tasks of each goal is to understand the difference between tasks you *can* do and tasks you *will* do. Nothing will get you off track faster or discourage you more (especially in the beginning) than to *bite off more than you can chew.*

Your next assignment is to write a biography of sorts. This will give you a clearer picture of where you are now and where you want to be in the future, hopefully, the *very near* future.

(Author's Note: Do not progress to the next chapter until you have completed all of the assignments in the previous one.)

Step 1: Write two paragraphs describing your life, career, and circumstances today.

Step 2: Write two paragraphs describing the vision you have for your career.

Step 3: Write two paragraphs describing the vision you have for your personal life.

Step 4: Make a list of the reasons why you chose a career in sales.

> ### *"Of all the words of tongue and pen, The saddest of all are—what might have been."*
>
> JOHN GREENLEAF WHITTIER

If you seem to be off track, or sometimes even at the wrong *station* when it comes to setting and achieving your goals, you may getting some *outside help*. Here are a few common success-saboteurs to avoid.

1. **Improper time management**

2. **Goals are not personalized**

3. **Negative self-talk/visualization**

4. **No step-by-step daily activity plan**

5. **No reward/penalty incentives**

6. **No quality time off = burnout**

7. **Short cutting (like moving on to the next chapter before completing your assignments in the previous one)**

8. **Not finishing what you start (see #7 above)**

9. **No progress analysis (inspecting what you expect)**

10. **Improper or lack of family/spouse support**

11. **Failure to delegate**

12. **Engaging in too many non-productive activities**

13. **Doing too many things at once = overload**

14. **Failure to take goal plan of action seriously**

15. **Letting others control your time**

16. **Improper or non-use of daily planner system**

17. **Unbalanced time (personal, professional, and family)**

Below are effective and proven goal setting techniques you can begin doing immediately to clearly identify your goals and begin creating a plan of action for their attainment.

Affirmation Statement
A written and concise *verbal* vision of what you want your family, personal, and professional life

to be like and exactly what must be done to achieve it. Read your affirmation statement aloud twice daily—once upon rising and again before retiring.

Affirmation Recording
This can be a direct reading from your affirmation statement as well as positive, motivational, and inspirational audio messages. The dialogue must be in first person and in your own voice. Use an enthusiastic and positive tone. Listen to the recording at least once a day. Modify it as needed.

Visualization
This is the ability to see yourself *beyond* your current circumstances. Visualization will work regardless of whether the input is positive or negative. You become what you think about all day long. You can practice visualization anywhere you have the chance to be alone with your thoughts. You have probably been engaging in some form of visualization most of your life. Most people refer to it as *day dreaming*. The difference is that with visualization, you are not merely fantasizing or hoping for a particular result or set of circumstances to occur. Visualization is a focused mental picture of exactly what you desire and exactly how you intend to attain it. You must see yourself *already* in possession of the desired results. You must see yourself doing everything it takes to achieve those results. The more detailed and precise the vision of your desires in your mind's eye, the greater affect it will have on your subconscious and conscious

mindsets—which will eventually exhibit themselves in external, physical realities.

Self-Talk
Also known as the voices within, it's something everyone engages in almost constantly. The key is to remember that those imaginary voices have very real consequences. They determine what we do (or don't do) on a daily basis—and how we spend our days *is* how we spend our lives. You must become aware of what those internal conversations are and the effect they are having on you. Then you must begin to make the necessary adjustments. But it all starts with *awareness*. The next time you find yourself engaging in negative or detrimental self-talk try this: Simply yell (not out loud) to yourself the word "STOP!" and throw that thought right out of your head and replace it with a pre-set positive thought. Easier said than done, but well worth the effort, especially if you can master the technique with any regularity.

Visuals
Collages and other visual aids are powerful tools to support and reinforce your visualization and affirmation exercises. It is just as important to *see* your goals as it is to hear them. Be sure to place your picture boards and visuals in a prominent location to be seen as often as possible.

Rewards and Penalties
The old carrot and stick is good enough for mules... good enough for us. Rewards and penalties are used as mental and physical incentives for goals

and tasks achieved or not achieved. The rewards can be for production or the activities toward the production. The size of the reward can vary from a new car to a jelly donut. It depends on the goal and the situation. Whether the stimulus is a reward or a penalty, the objective is the same—to reinforce your commitment to the goal or objective. Whether it is a reward or a penalty, it must be *immediate* to be fully effective. Time diminishes the impact.

Associations

Be careful of the associations and relationships you develop. If there is a group within the office whose primary activities include non-business and socializing interaction with their co-workers, you may wish to avoid them altogether. You may also wish to do the same with individual associations as well, especially among low producers, negative personality types, and the like.

Failure by association—*Eagles don't hang out in duck ponds.*

Thoughts

Thoughts are things. Treat them as such. As I've said before, we become what we think about all day long. Please pay special attention to the following words and take them to heart, as I did many years ago.

> *"Watch your thoughts, for they become words.*
> *Watch your words, for they become actions.*

Watch your actions, for they become habits.
Watch your habits, for they become your character.
Watch your character, for it becomes your destiny."

FRANK OUTLAW

Here are some things to remember when identifying your goals and the structured plan for their attainment. It's not enough just to *write them down*. Don't simply make a list and mail it in. Remember, when it comes to getting what you want...*you* are Santa Claus.

Your goals must be real, personal, attainable, positive, and above all...*acted upon.*

Many of your goals are going to be material in nature. In other words, they'll require money to attain. When developing your annual budget for your goals, there are some things to keep in mind to avoid biting off more than you can chew, financially speaking. Nothing will discourage you more than seeing no noticeable progress toward your goals or ability to attain them.

Money is going to be the primary limiting force when it comes to your material goals. Therefore, plan for its acquisition in sufficient quantity, as well as its proper use and management.

1. **Your annual budget must be sufficient to support all of your expenses.**

2. Your annual budget must be sufficient to incorporate all of the personal, family, and professional goals you have set.

3. Review previous years' expenses, budget, tax returns, and so on, to develop an accurate projection of what lies ahead this year.

4. Include lifestyle expenses—*toys*, dining out, hobbies, club memberships, and so on.

5. Allow for high expense periods such as Christmas and vacations.

6. Allow for savings and investments.

7. Include time saving expenses—gardener, pool maintenance, housekeeping, and the like.

When it comes to the acquisition and management of money, working hard and hoping for the best doesn't work for two reasons. First, that isn't a plan; it's a statement. Second, you don't get ahead by working *harder*. You get ahead by working *smarter*. Here are some things to keep in mind when developing your goal setting and plan of action.

1. When it's all said and done, you don't get what you *want* in life, so much as you get what you *are*. So make one of your goals to *become* the person you need to become to get what you want in life.

2. For every goal, there is a way to achieve it. For every problem, there is a solution.

3. Put it in writing! And read it out loud often!

4. A written plan keeps you focused and gives you direction.

5. A written plan let's you break the overall goal into attainable sections / tasks.

6. A written plan let's you track results and project forward.

7. A written plan reduces the risk of failure (by 90 percent).

8. Schedule a meeting with your family and significant others to develop a business plan that incorporates *their* personal goals as well. Make a family *wish list* so to speak and ideally enlist their help in attaining those goals.

9. When visualizing the successful results of your plan, remember to not just *see* the results, but see yourself *already in possession* of those results as well.

"We've got to have a dream if we are going to make a dream come true."

DENIS E. WAITLEY

CHAPTER 7: TIME MANAGEMENT

$

"Don't serve time. Make time serve you."

<small>WILLIE SUTTON (BANK ROBBER)</small>

A man stood upon a mountain top and yelled to the universe, "Give me more time!" At which point the universe replied back, "There is no more time. Give me more *you*."

When it comes to finding the time to do the things we want in addition to the things we must, it seems we never find the time to do both—at least not as effectively as we'd like. That's why you have to *make* the time, *manage* the time, and *prioritize* the time.

Here are a few techniques for helping you make, manage, and prioritize your time more effectively.

1. **Set a specific time each day to review your written goal plan of action.**

2. **Manage your busy work effectively. Don't let it manage you.**

3. **Prioritize tasks and duties constantly.**

4. **Be flexible—stuff happens.**

5. **Be aware of** *time bandits*.

6. **Learn to say "no."**

7. **Eliminate procrastination—just do it!**

8. **Learn to delegate minor or unproductive tasks.**

9. **Utilize** *prime times* **(explained later).**

10. **Utilize** *down times* **effectively.**

11. **Have an "I'm working. Do not disturb" attitude while at the office.**

12. **Do the highest priority tasks first, then work your way down the list.**

13. **Properly prepare for tasks before beginning them.**

You need to start seeing and treating time for what it really is—the most valuable resource you have or will ever have! You can *spend* time; you can *invest* time; you can *waste* time; you can even *save* time, but you cannot *replace* time. How often have you heard someone say, "*If I only had it to do over again.*" Let me tell you something. It's a lot easier to take the time to do something right the first time then it is to go back and fix it later. If you are anything like me, then you've already discovered that the *short* cut often ends up being the *long* or *wrong* cut.

The only way to manage your time effectively on an hourly/daily basis is to maintain your written schedule using a daily planner system, because first, our memory stinks, and second, the most effective way to control and manage your time is to *organize* it. Ask the most successful salespeople you know if they use a written daily planner system and you'll find that nearly all of them will tell you they do.

A written daily planner system is not simply a list of your scheduled appointments. It is a complete time management system that guides your activities on a successful path to attain the goals you have set. Your planner system incorporates all of the activities you must complete in order to achieve the productivity standards you have set for yourself.

Think of your daily planner system as your own success kit that includes a calendar.

That same formula for success applies to taking control of and properly managing your time as well. Just as your success is up to you, if *you* don't control your time, others will. Taking control of your time is, for most of us, something we have been trained *against* most of our lives. Think about it. We first started out on our parent's schedule. Then we moved on to our teacher's schedule, then on to our employer's schedule. When was the last time you were in complete control of any major portion of your time?

So how do you begin to take back total control of your time? By taking your time *seriously*. If you don't take your time seriously, how can you expect others to? When I was running one of the largest real estate offices in North America I began to notice an alarming trend among my staff when it came to taking charge of their schedules. In the typical real estate office, the entire sales force is comprised of *independent contractors*. To management, this means simply that the agents pay their own taxes. To the sales staff, it means they cannot be forced to do *anything* that will make them successful.

As *independent* contractors who can't be told what to do, it was my job as manager to tell them anyway. Time does not stop; it is constantly evaporating right before our eyes. If you do not manage and control your time, someone else will.

When the average salesperson enters the profession for the first time, it is usually from a career that involved a more structured time schedule (nine to five). His family and those around him, as well as the salesperson, grew to accept this fact as a matter of economic survival. As a result, the household's schedule was dictated by the breadwinner's schedule—which was controlled by the breadwinner's employer.

You've probably been a part of a household whose schedule was dictated and controlled by outside factors such as a parent's employer. Everyone's schedule revolved around the time-frame set by the employer, who probably set that schedule with little or no regard to the needs of the household or the employee. The family would not schedule dinner at five o'clock if the parent(s) didn't get off work until six. If a family member was to encounter a parent sitting on the couch at noon watching TV when he was supposed to be at work, even that child would sense something was wrong. Why? Because she would know and respect the parent's schedule and notice when the parent wasn't doing the same. *Aren't you supposed to be at work right now?*

But some tragic metamorphosis takes place when that same individual goes from punching a clock to being totally in charge of their own schedule. It's as if his time no longer has the same value as it did when it was controlled by someone else.

The main problem, in addition to the salesperson diminishing the value of his own time, is that fact that those around him followed the salesperson's example. When one of my real estate salespeople would complain to me that his family was making greater demands on his time now that he was *free to come go as he pleased,* I would ask, "And where do you supposed they got that concept from?" When you take your schedule seriously, others will too. It's hard to get others to value something of *yours* when you don't seem to value it *yourself.*

"Set priorities for your goals...a major part of successful living lies in the ability to put first things first. Indeed, the reason most major goals are not achieved is that we spend our time doing second things first."

ROBERT J. MCKAIN

"To the world you may be one person, but to one person you may be the world." MAHATMA GANDI

Trying to operate a successful business without the proper support of your family or significant others is like playing golf with a dead body... dragging it from hole to hole. I've golfed with people who played like they were dead, but at least they carried their own clubs.

During the chapter on goal setting, I suggested when putting together a list of objectives to include your spouse, family, and significant others in the development, planning, and attainment of as many of your goals as possible. If done properly, you and they will notice that many, if not all of your goals will be mutually beneficial to your circle. If they're made to understand that you attaining *your* goals directly benefits *them*, they will be more inclined (even enthusiastic) about not only supporting and encouraging you, but also actually assisting in the required tasks to obtain those goals.

Together **E**ach **A**chieves **M**ore.

We talked about the progress, no matter how small, you must continually make toward your objectives. We also discussed how progress (change) can be difficult at times. It often requires tough decisions on your part. Some of those decisions will alter the course of your life from that moment on. For instance, you may have to make the decision to focus more of your time and energy on a certain aspect of your life or new relationships, which will undoubtedly come at the expense of other aspects and relationships.

Sometimes success is defined by what we had to give up to achieve it.

As I described earlier, one fear sometimes associated with individuals seeking success is a fear of achieving that success they supposedly are seeking. One symptom of those who may be harboring some fear or hesitancy about being *super successful* is an income level within 10 percent of their immediate circle's income level. Birds of a feather....

Obtaining all of the success you desire may sometimes mean alienating or even parting altogether with that established inner circle of friends and family. You may be saying to yourself right now that your family and/or spouse would be tickled pink if you suddenly became "super successful." But that is an assumption I've seen all too often be wrong. Oh, at first the extra freedom and benefits can be a complete blessing, but like I said, with change comes problems.

My point is this; when one of you starts succeeding at a greater level than the others in your *circle*, one of three things is probably going to happen: one, they will have to make the trip with you; two, they will be left behind; three, you will stay behind with them.

One of the best ways to enlist the enthusiastic support and participation of your friends and family in achieving your goals is to enthusiastically support and participate in the achieving of *their* goals.

This will not only personalize your goals to you but it will also make your goals have personal meaning to them as well. For instance, they may no longer see it as you working late *again*. They now see those extra hours at the office as that family vacation next summer. It's not working weekends at the office. It's that new bicycle or new car. I'm not saying *buy them off*. I'm saying buy them *in*—1 + 1 = 3 when it's a good partnership. So get them *onboard* in the beginning and maybe you won't have to throw them *overboard* later.

Here are a few tips you can use to help gain the *enthusiastic* support of your spouse, family, and significant others.

1. **Arrange a** *special* **family meeting. Make sure everyone knows that this meeting is significant for** *all* **of them. Use the meeting to plan every individual's as well as the group's goals, plans of action, and time frames for their attainment. Use all the goal-setting techniques learned**

in chapter six. The key is to create excitement and com-mitment from the group.

2. Be sure that everyone understands that a career in sales, while at times may be flexible, is still demanding and time consuming to be successful, usually more so than other careers. There are going to be times when despite your best efforts and intentions, you're going to have to work late, or weekends, or miss dinner unexpectedly. You have to get them on board mentally to accept and deal with the fact that a successful career in sales can, at times, re-sult in you not being *there* in order to be somewhere else accomplishing the family's goals. If that doesn't work, you can always say, "I told you this might happen!"

3. **Put it in writing!** When conducting my *SELL LIKE CRAZY* sales professional training workshops, I provide a con-tract to be signed by all members of the participant's family, circle, and so on. Then I make them return it with all the signatures and make copies for all parties. I call it the *Support Agreement.* And that's what it is, an *agreement* by all parties to give the necessary support, understanding, encouragement, feedback, and flex-ibility, with each party pledging to do his/her part and to assist the others in doing their parts.

4. Remind everyone that self confidence is often dictated by what we hear others say about and to us. So, what are you *hearing* from your friends and family. Is it, "You can!" or is it, "Can you?" Just make sure everyone un-derstands the impact words have on a person's attitude and feelings about himself, and how, as a sales profes-sional, what you hear from those around you can im-

pact your performance and state of mind, which are the two primary factors that will determine your success and income in this business.

5. Make sure everyone is aware that *little things* have a way of quickly morphing into big things. One straw at a time broke the camel's back! Just as *little* words of encouragement can have a big impact on us, so too can little words or actions of discouragement. Many will slip by unnoticed but their impact will be felt nonetheless. The key here is *communication*. For instance, if you feel that your spouse is saying or doing something that may be having an adverse effect on your state of mind, then communicate your feelings. Let him or her know that while you do appreciate their input, you would like it to be more positive and constructive when possible. Explain to them why this is necessary and how it benefits *them*. But also keep in mind that once in a while you're going to have to let them unload on you. Sorry.

6. Make sure everyone is aware of the fact that despite your best intentions and efforts to the contrary, your home life affects your personal life, and vice versa. I'm sure you've worked with more than a few individuals who could never quite keep their private lives private. I'm sure you also noticed that, more often than not, it had an effect on their job performance. Well, the opposite scenario also holds true. Things that happen at the office cannot always be left *at* the office. Your support circle must understand that maybe a thirty-minute decompression period is needed after you arrive home from the office, especially during periods of heavy activity and demands.

7. **Establish regularly scheduled days off. No exceptions! Your family must believe that you** *work to live*, **and not the other way around. The candle burns quickest when lit at both ends. Pace yourself, and use the time off to recharge your batteries, so to speak. You'll find that not only does your personal and family life benefit, but your professional one will as well. Place your** *personal* **obligations at the top of your list. It's the key to a long and happy life.**

8. **Invite your family and spouse to as many company/ professional functions as possible. Let them see exactly who and what you deal with on a daily basis. The best way to get them on your side is to get them involved in what your side is doing. Believe me, when your job has a** *face* **to it, they will be more understanding and supportive when things go wrong, and there will be times when you need that extra understanding and support.**

If this chapter hasn't put your personal and professional relationships into perspective, maybe this will. When Gugliemo Marconi, credited as the inventor of the radio, told everyone he had invented a system of sending electrical transmissions through the air without the use of wires, his competitors were awed and impressed. His family and friends, on the other hand, had him committed to an insane asylum.

"Who has not served cannot command."

JOHN FLORIO

CHAPTER 9: SELF IMAGE

"We have met the enemy...and they are us."
WALT KELLY

Fifty percent of the people you meet will judge you *entirely* by your appearance. An additional 25 five percent will judge you *in part* by your appearance. That means 75 percent of the people you meet will make a judgment about you before you even open your mouth!

When dealing with the public, especially in your role as a salesperson, the outward physical image and appearance you present is the determining factor in how you and your message are received. This may seem a bit superficial, but it's a fact of any *people* business.

At certain times, when dealing with certain individuals and situations, you may have to project varying images depending on the particular client or situation. The most successful salespeople will always tailor their image, to a certain degree, to better appeal to their clients. For instance, as a realtor, I would always be sure to dress accordingly, depending upon the type of property/client I was dealing with at the time. I would always wear

85

my best suit when showing high-end properties. On the other hand, I would not wear a suit or even a tie when showing rural properties.

I tried to tailor my message to increase its appeal to the client by first tailoring my image and appearance in a way I felt would be more appealing. I knew if the client first liked what he "saw," he would be more inclined to like what he was about to *hear*. If his initial impression of me was not one that inspired confidence and likeability, then anything I did or said after that would be diminished. Clients seldom listen to salespeople they don't trust and they seldom trust anyone they don't like.

More sales have been lost because the salesperson dressed for failure instead of dressing for success.

We discussed earlier the importance of creating the proper *self-image* by effectively crafting your *outer-image*. Remember, most of us see ourselves based at least in part on how we perceive others see us. Your outward appearance is the first place to start when trying to develop and project the proper image.

I once managed a real estate office that had an agent working there who never seemed to wear anything other than short pants and a T-shirt. Despite his casual appearance, he was quite successful, plus, we were located in Southern California (not really known for its formal attire standards). One day, I asked him if he would start wearing at least long pants while in the office—a shirt and tie wouldn't be a bad idea either. His response was, "My clients don't mind." My answer to that was, "Well maybe *our* clients *do*."

When you are in a professional situation, not only *act* like it, but *look* like it as well. Did you notice I said *professional situation* and not just at the office or around clients? I used to work a great deal from my home and I found that I accomplished twice as much, and was twice as effective over the phone when I was dressed in some kind of business attire (as opposed to a bathrobe and Dodgers cap). As Yogi Berra said, "Ninety percent of this game is half mental," even when no one is watching.

I will discuss in greater detail how to project a more successful image through communication and appearance in the chapter on "Effective Communication," but for now, here are some tips on projecting a more professional and competent image through a few minor adjustments in your outward physical appearance.

1. **Proper fitting and coordinated suit/outfit**

2. **Avoid excessive jewelry**

3. **Quality watch**

4. **Buttons buttoned/none missing**

5. **Shoes shined**

6. **Unbitten, clean, trimmed finger nails**

7. **Head and facial hair neatly trimmed**

8. **Clean and pressed clothing**

Some of these things may seem ridiculously obvious to *you*, but not to many of the salespeople I've managed over the years.

When you are writing contracts that are going to cost someone money, especially on high ticket items, you better believe all eyes in the room are on *you*, and your *hands* as well. If you bite your nails, the client may notice. Nail biting can be interpreted as a sign of nervousness or *lack of confidence*.

I can't tell you how many times I've sat across the negotiating table with a so called cool and calm professional with nails bitten down to the nub. Or seen a salesperson hand a client the pen to sign over a great deal of money, with dirt under his fingernails or wearing clothes that look like they were slept in.

First, you "see" it; then you "believe" it; then you "achieve" it. The same is true for creating the proper self image. And it all starts with what you "see" when you look in the mirror. Keep in mind, just because we see ourselves in a certain way does not mean that others will see us that way. Often, we are much more critical of ourselves than anyone else could ever be. If you have a good feeling about yourself, you are more prone to believe that others share the same opinion. Therefore, you are more likely to live up to that opinion.

Who is usually the best dressed person in your office/organization? They are your new dress code standard. Your goal is to replace them as the best dressed as soon as your budget allows.

> *"You have no idea what a poor opinion I have of myself...and how little I deserve it."*
>
> W.S. GILBERT

SECTION 3: The Business of Sales

"Selling is the easiest business in the world—if you eliminate all the others."

PHIL KREIDER

CHAPTER 10: THE BUSINESS

"Choose a job you love and you'll never have to work a day in your life." — CONFUCIUS

The sales industry must love failures—since it has created so many of them.

It takes a very special type of person to succeed in a field with such a high attrition rate. Proving what many of you already know, not everyone has what it takes to be a successful salesperson. That's just the way it is. A career in sales often involves out-smarting and out-working your competition—not an easy task. It involves getting people to part with their hard earned money—an even harder task.

Speaking of hard earned money, what is your income goal for the next twelve months? Let's use $50,000 for the purposes of this illustration. Instead of *you* being the one earning the fifty grand a year, I ask you to put yourself in the shoes of your employer, the one *paying* the $50,000. If you were going to pay someone the amount of money per year that you want to be paid, would it matter to you how many hours per week that person worked? I mean *really* worked, not just time at the office. Would it matter to you how that person conducted himself while at your office? How he dressed? How he interacted with the other salespeople? Would it matter to you if that person committed to and achieved his production goals? Of course it would! That's why employers invented job descriptions, dress codes, office policies, performance quotas, and everything else you probably thought they just made up to stifle your creativity.

The first question you must ask yourself is would you pay *you* what you now earn, for doing what you do, if that money was coming out of your pocket instead of going into it? In other words, is your current employer getting their money's worth? If the answer wasn't an enthusiastic "Yes," don't worry. This book is going to teach you how to become a bargain employee at any price!

If you have any reservations about your career in sales at this point, I'd be willing to bet those concerns are more directed toward *yourself* as opposed to the business. Granted, not *everyone* can be a successful salesperson...but *anyone* can if he is willing to do what "everyone" else won't.

The first thing you have to get away from is this *natural born salesperson* concept. Professional salespeople are built one sale at a time.

I have seen just a single setback utterly destroy some salespeople—ones I thought had very prom-

ising futures. I've seen salespeople pass up training opportunities where they might have learned
something that could have literally turned their career around. You just don't wake up one day and
say, "I can no longer be a successful salesperson."
You get there over a period of days, days that turn
into weeks, and weeks that turn into months. I've
seen some salespeople have a slump that lasted
the rest of their career!

The biggest enemy of anyone in the field of sales
is complacency. Complacency can destroy a career faster than any negative market conditions
or competitor ever could. Once again, complacency is not something you just wake up with one
day. It's a *process*. It takes *time*, and it has warning signs that you can recognize and, hopefully,
avoid.

Complacency begins by taking for granted things
that should warrant greater attention. I view it as
falling asleep at the switch. After engaging in almost any activity over a period of time, a certain
amount of apathy and indifference is going to set
in. This is common. Unfortunately, just as common
is the fact that the chains of habit are often too
weak to be felt until they are too strong to be broken. And before you know it, it's too late to avoid
the iceberg.

The first stage of career complacency is *apathy*—
often regardless of the level of success achieved.
What the salesperson once enjoyed, he now

views as burdensome or boring. The next phase is *acceptance*. That's where the effort it takes to reverse course seems to outweigh the negatives of staying in your comfort zone. After a while, "things don't seem so bad." The next phase is the real killer—*justification*.

Regardless of the career you choose, especially if it's one in sales, there is going to be a certain amount of frustration and burnout involved. In fact, how many people do you know right now who are at their jobs doing nothing more than the bare minimum to collect their paycheck each week? How many people do you know right now who are passionate about their work? What are the differences in those two group's incomes? More importantly, which group seems happier?

Take a career in sales casually and you will end up a *casualty*.

Many are called, but few are chosen. A career in sales has one of the highest attrition rates of any occupation, and a primary cause of that attrition (even ahead of the stress factor) is lack of sufficient income. There is an old joke that goes: a guy won ten million dollars in the lottery and decided to pursue a career in sales until the money ran out.

Many people are drawn to a career in sales because they envision big and easy money. Those of you already in this business probably realize this is a fallacy. If you are looking for *short hours and big paychecks*, then I suggest you look elsewhere. Doing the minimum required to succeed in this business may keep you *up* with the competition, but doing just that little extra will keep you *ahead* of the competition.

Now I am going to give you the formula for success regardless of what your individual sales career is: *Enthusiasm plus the basics*. That's it. When the going gets tough, the tough get back to the basics.

I often use the terms *"job"* or *"career"* in sales. Let me clarify that. A career in sales isn't so much a job or career as much as it is a *lifestyle*. In fact, I view the business of sales as the *game of life*. Everything you need to succeed in life can be learned from a career in sales. The same attitude, people skills, self-motivation strategies, goal setting, and time management techniques (and just about everything else) that are necessary to succeed in sales are also necessary for a successful life in general.

The business of sales can be one of the greatest learning experiences of your entire life. It has been for me. Developing the habits and principles it takes to be successful in sales often carries over to your personal life as well, often with the same results. The systems and processes that I am teaching you in this book work, regardless of the circumstances to which they are applied. As I said earlier, success is a *process*.

There may be a million ways to fail at a career in sales. But there is not one excuse! Anyone can become a successful sales professional if they are willing to put in the time and effort—not *everyone*, but anyone.

Because I do not know your *specific* circumstances, let me give you some *general* advice. *If you worry about your job, you'll never have to worry about your job.* Anything worth spending your valuable time doing is worth doing to the best of your ability, regardless of who you are, who you work for, or what you get paid. When the day comes when you no longer have the drive and enthusiasm to give it your clients your best, find a new line of work.

> **"I used to sell furniture for a living. The trouble was, it was my own."**
>
> LES DAWSON

$

"It's not how much it's worth. It's how much people think it's worth." — HARVEY MACKAY

Who makes the best *selling* hamburgers? Who makes the best *tasting* hamburgers? Did you give the same answer to both questions?

Wouldn't *logic* dictate that the best *tasting* hamburger would also be the best *selling*? Absolutely. So why isn't the best tasting hamburger also the best selling? Because logic has very little to do with selling. Regardless of the quality of the product, there are at least four *greater* reasons why consumers choose one product over another.

The first reason consumers commonly prefer or choose to purchase a particular product or service over another is *convenience*—not only convenient to *use* but convent to *purchase* as well. The easier it is for the customer to purchase the product, the more often he will. I see so many items that I would use, many on a regular basis, but I simply don't have the time or the inclination to jump through all the hoops of the seller's system of purchase. The last thing buyers of the "I want it now" generation are looking for is to complete some kind manual dexterity test in order to acquire the product—regardless of quality or price.

Not all salespeople are lucky enough to be selling products that actually sell themselves, or that consumers must purchase as a necessity. Everything else requires a higher level of salesmanship, as well as convenience to increase sales. An example is selling a product that requires assembly. Statistics have shown that products requiring assembly sell in far less quantities than the same product available pre-assembled. Many companies have found that paying the extra small cost of assembling the product pre-sale is more than offset by larger profits from increased sales.

Of course, this may not always be an option. If the product itself cannot help reduce the level of effort by the consumer, there may be other things you can do to make it easier to *purchase*, or at the very *least*, find when customers need to. The easier you make your product or service to locate and acquire, the more buyers you're going to attract and the more sales you're going to make. Not to mention the fact that if you make your product or service easy to locate and acquire, the less likely the customer will be to mind any other difficulties associated with it. If there is any part of your selling chain that is complicated, then you need to over-compensate by making other aspects of its purchase easier. The customers will notice.

The first place to start creating a system that makes it easier for your buyers to buy is at the source—the customer. Before you begin *telling* them how *you* sell, start by *asking* them how *they* prefer to buy? It's just that simple—*ask them*. You may be surprised at what they've been trying to tell you all along.

One of the best ways to immediately identify any preferences your buyers may have is to "ask them" in a formal manner such as survey. Retailers use them on customers all the time. Why do you suppose they do that? Trust me, it's not because they're *just curious*. They have a reason.

My advice is to not limit your surveys to just the people you'll be selling *to*. Be sure to include those you sell *with* and *for*. It's very important to include others who are a part of the selling chain. Survey anyone who has an even remote awareness of, or need for, your product or service…maybe even the janitorial staff at your office.

That last suggestion may sound like a joke, but it's not. I once owned an interest in an automotive dealership. As to not interfere with the daily operations of the car lot, we would have the cars detailed and washed in the evenings after normal business hours. While conducting a quality service survey of all our customers and staff, *including the evening auto detailing crew*, I discovered something remarkable when reviewing the questionnaires of the cleaning crew—which, by the way, according to my *sales* manager, was a "waste of time."

The remarkable thing I discovered was that after our normal business hours, after everyone except the cleaning crew had gone home for the day, at least ten people per night would stop by the dealership to check out some of the vehicles. They would sometimes even ask if they could leave a deposit with one of the detailing crew to hold the car until we opened the following day. The cleaning crew of course had no more authority than to tell them to return during business hours. Anyone involved in the field of sales will tell you, *He who hesitates is lost*…and we were losing potentially ten sales a day. You must strike while the iron is hot!

Of all the people who stopped by in the evening and were told to return during business hours, only a fraction of them did so. In the car sales business, that's called, "Letting the money walk off the lot."

Where do you suppose that money "walked off" to? The competition! Those customers didn't suddenly decide they no longer wanted to purchase a new car simply because we were closed. That money went right out of my pocket and directly into the pockets of those doing everything they could to put me out of business. That's called giving aid and comfort to the enemy.

Who knows how many of those *potential* clients could have been converted to *real* clients had they been speaking to a trained salesperson rather than one of the cleaning personnel? Once this startling revelation was discovered, we began extending our normal business hours, and immediately increased our sales production by 12 percent, 12 percent that went into *my* pocket rather than my competitors.

When it comes to the product or service you are offering, you must realize that in the eyes of your customers, *you* are the expert. They often believe you know, *or should know*, everything there is about the product or service, and expect you to correctly and honestly answer any questions regarding it; that is, until you say or do something that completely blows your credibility or tells them otherwise.

If you talk to any top professional in the field of sales, I believe you will discover they indeed *are* the expert regarding their product or service. They *do* know everything about the product—at least everything they *need* to know about it. They are also able to answer any questions or address any concerns the customer might have nine out of ten times.

What about the one out of ten times they don't know? They usually do the next best thing, admit they don't know. The mark of a true salesperson is his ability to find a reason to call or come back if he can't make the sale then and there. To most salespeople the words, "I don't know" can be the kiss of death, but to the trained professional it's another opportunity to follow up and stay in touch with the client. *"That's a good question; I'll find out the answer and get back to you."*

But like I said, that is "the *next* best thing." Remember, the *best* thing is still to know the answer (and make the sale) in the first place.

I mentioned the importance of making your product or service as easy to buy as possible. This goes hand in hand with product knowledge. Your inability to address a concern of the client adequately could cost you the sale, even if the customer's concern is unfounded or wrong. It doesn't always benefit you to have a reason to call or come back if the client is ready to buy *now*.

Let's say you walk into an auto parts store looking for a part for your car. You ask the person behind the counter (fellow brother in sales) if he has the particular part in stock. The salesperson says he's not sure and will have to get back to you.

Now what do you do? Go home and wait for them to call? Of course not. You go to the next auto parts store and make your purchase *there*. You give store number two the money that store number one let "walk off the lot." Product knowledge and salesmanship go hand in hand.

Unskilled or unknowledgeable salespeople can cost a lot more than they get paid. Some salespeople can be had for minimum wage and yet still cost a fortune to employ.

The best way to get the public to buy what you're selling is to sell what the public is buying."

Sell what's selling may sound like a no-brainer. But are you selling what's selling in *sufficient quantities* to achieve the goals you listed in the earlier chapter? Will it take more effort or time to reach those goals selling your current product or service than it would another? The *best* covered wagon in the world still would not outsell today's *worst* automobile. Why? Because we are living in an *automotive* age. People are still buying gas-guzzlers regardless of the benefits of owning a mode of transportation that runs on no gas at all. Are you selling covered wagons in this day and age?

Hopefully, you enjoy what you're selling and, hopefully, so do your customers. If you believe in your product or service, your customers will be more inclined to do so as well. When your customers start believing in you and what you are offering, they will be more inclined to buy what you're selling. This means the more you believe in what you're selling, the more you'll sell of it. Therefore, don't automatically pick a sales job that offers the highest commission products or services. Yes, sell what's selling, and sell what you can sell in sufficient quantities to achieve your production and income goals, but from that group, choose the product or service that you would *enjoy* selling the most, regardless if it's the highest paying product or service.

What you lose in the *quality* of *your* commissions, your enthusiasm for the product should make up for in the *quantity* of your sales. Like I said, selling is *always* a numbers game no matter how you look at it. The key is to make those numbers work *for* you and not *against* you.

My challenge to you right now is to become the *expert* regarding your particular product or service. Believe me, not only will your customers benefit from this, but so will you. Take a closer look at what you have been offering and what you *could* be offering. There's always room for improvement...just ask your customers.

"Who the hell wants to hear Actors talk?"

H.M. Warner, Founder of Warner
Brothers Pictures, 1927

"We don't like their sound, and guitar music is on the way out."

Decca Recording Studios rejecting
the Beatles, 1962

"This 'telephone' has too many shortcomings to be seriously considered as a means of communication. This device is inherently of no value to us."

Western Union internal memo, 1876

"You say this is a computer for ordinary people? Why would an ordinary person want a computer?"

STEVE WOZNIAK REGARDING THE APPLE PROTOTYPE

"I think there is a world market for maybe 5 computers."

THOMAS WATSON, CHAIRMAN OF IBM, 1943

"The concept is interesting and well formed, but to earn better than a 'C' the idea must be feasible."

A YALE UNIVERSITY MANAGEMENT PROFESSOR'S RESPONSE TO FRED SMITH'S PAPER PROPOSING A RELIABLE OVER-NIGHT DELIVERY SERVICE. (SMITH WENT ON TO BECOME FOUNDER OF FEDERAL EXPRESS.)

CHAPTER 12: THE MARKET

$

"Here is a simple and powerful rule...always give people more than they expect to get." NELSON BOSWELL

I t is rumored a newspaper reporter once asked famed bank robber Willie Sutton why he robbed banks. Willie replied, "Because that's where the money is!" You could say that Willie Sutton knew his market place. And of course, he had a pretty effective sales tool as well.

One concept we covered in the last chapter was to *"sell what's selling."* This chapter will detail how to sell *where* it's selling. In other words, *putting your mouth where your money is.*

There are three factors that define the market-place: one, the product; two, the consumer; and three, the salesperson. Yes, the *salesperson*! This is where it might actually pay to *stay* in your comfort zone.

Sometimes, as salespeople, our market place is chosen for us by our employer, regardless of our knowledge or comfort level. The key to sales is gaining *new* markets while still maintaining and increasing the existing ones, which means you're always going to be infiltrating unfamiliar territory to expand your market. Once you establish yourself in a "new" market, it then becomes an "existing" one. A salesperson always has a higher level of knowledge and comfort when prospecting in familiar territory. Therefore, learn *the lay of the land* as fast as possible when entering new markets. Time is crucial in the beginning. The sales will come if you *first* establish the sufficient level of knowledge and comfort in your market.

If your marketing plan includes an introductory period at the beginning, as you become more familiar with your market and consumers, be sure to account for lower than expected production during this first phase (down-time). You'll make it up down the road as those relationships come to fruition. Many salespeople get off to a great start in their market area and successfully gain the trust of their client base, but get discouraged and abandon that market before their early groundbreaking efforts have a chance to begin paying dividends.

There are basically two types of general markets—geographic and demographic. Demographic means your market is a group of individuals, and geographic means your market is where those individuals are located. For instance, if your industry sells child safety products, then your *demographic* market place would be adults with small children or those who care for them. If your product happens to be earthquake insurance then your *geo-graphic* market would be the entire west coast of the United States.

The most successful marketing campaigns will often be a combination of both. The more specific and targeted your marketing efforts are, the more calculable the results will be. If you've had the luxury of choosing your own market place, then hopefully you've chose one that you are familiar and comfortable with, and somewhat knowledgeable about. If on the other hand your market place has chosen *you*...then your immediate goal is to *become* familiar and comfortable with, and knowledgeable about, it—and with the help of this book, very successful in it.

Once a potential market has been identified, it must then be *analyzed*. The key is to obtain as much data and information about your market as possible, even before you proceed to making direct contact with it. It must be studied. Your goal is to gain a *working knowledge* of your customers, their buying environment, habits, and preferences.

When it comes to understanding your market, the first thing to *understand* is the only thing permanent is change. By the time you learn everything you can about your market, it will have changed. That's why it's so hard for any one provider to *corner the market*, because there are no corners. It's one big oval track constantly in motion with new products, services, sellers, and buyers constantly jockeying for position. And the position you'll be jockeying for is number one.

The best way for you to gain and maintain that number one pole position in your market is to become the *go-to provider* of your particular service or product. All eyes are always on the lead horse. Everyone watching knows who the lead horse is and where they are in regard to the track and the other horses.

To use the above analogy, you are the Jockey; your product/service is the horse; the track is your market; the other horses are your competitors; and the fans in the stands are your customers. You win the race by out smarting or outperforming the other jockeys and by conquering the track (market) and the conditions it presents at any given time. Understanding and believing in your horse (product) doesn't hurt either.

Favorable track conditions benefit all the horses. The fans in the stands have no impact on the race and the other jockeys are going to run their own race. Regardless of the market or the customer, it still comes down to the salesperson and product (jockey and horse). The good news is that those are the only two things you have complete control over. Or are you just along for the ride? Remember, just because you seem to be moving fast in the right direction, getting dragged by one foot ain't horseback riding.

Market conditions dictate buying conditions and buying conditions dictate selling conditions. Therefore, if buying is a process then so is selling.

Once you have identified a potential market place, created an awareness and understanding of it, and how you as a salesperson will interact with it. You must then begin formulating a plan of action to achieve your objectives within it. Again, those activities that comprise your plan will unfold as part of a process, a "process" that probably won't happen overnight or without a few setbacks along the way. So plan accordingly.

I'm assuming your goal eventually will be market saturation to the point where you are the number one provider of your particular product or service in your particular market area. Start by first gaining the attention of your consumers. If you successfully do that, you'll soon attract the attention of your competitors. That leaves you a small window of opportunity to fly under the radar and establish some kind of beachhead before the competition gets you in their sights. That's why it's so crucial to apply as much effort and resources as possible when first entering a new market place. The first shot is always the most crucial because you can't take it back and it gives away your position and intentions. So make it count. You may even catch some competitors so unawares that you greatly damage or even cripple them altogether. The more small fish you knock out in the first round, the more effort and resources you can direct at the big fish when they start to arrive.

Just be sure that whatever plan you have for your competition is ready and in place *before* you fire that first shot. After that, they tend to start shooting back. *Striking* first doesn't always mean *shooting* first, then asking questions later. The first step should always be to develop a plan of action to deal with your competitors before they develop a plan to deal with you. You'll never get a second chance to be the *new gun* in town. After that, you'll always have a target on your back.

There are five important steps to gaining and maintaining new markets. Whether they be geographic or demographic, dominated by competitors or wide open, the process is still the same: identify, enter, establish, conquer, defend, expand.

1. **Identify: That means the market as well as your approach to it. What do you hope to accomplish, and at what cost? What are the time frames and resources involved? Is your goal the whole market or only a specific piece of it? Another key factor is of course whose market is it *now* and how will they react to you entering it. You must be able to identify and successfully deal with your competition and any counter attacks they launch. Basically, what you need to identify is what you want and how you plan to get it while taking into account what others will do to stop you.**

2. **Enter: You must have a written plan of action, *and* it must be one that accomplishes the desired results. Remember, General Custer had a plan. The Donner party had a plan. Even the Titanic had a plan. The problem was that**

their plans for achieving success didn't include planning for avoiding failure. Planning for failure *is* planning for success. Custer at Little Big Horn, the Donner Party, and the Titanic were all disasters that could have been easily avoided had there been a plan in place for at least the possibility of failure.

My suggestion is to concentrate 80 percent of your resources and effort during your initial entry into the market, saving 20 percent for reserves and counter-measures. Resources and effort may need to be higher when attacking heavily defended and established markets. The key is to make a big splash and gain momentum quickly until you become entrenched.

If there's any market worth going after, you're probably not going to be the first one to realize it, or the first to do something about it. Therefore, more often than not you will have to either create a place at the table for yourself or kick somebody out of theirs, or both.

Once your presence in the dining hall is made known, the element of surprise is now gone. The other *diners* are going to have to deal with you one way or the other and do their best to keep you from eating what's on their plate.

As I explained earlier, there is no reality; there is only *perceived* reality. So what do you do if you can't make a big splash right away? Give the *perception* of one—also known as psychological warfare. The ancient Roman soldiers were masters at creating an illusion of superiority on the battlefield, even when it was just that—an *illusion*. If you have ever seen an accurate portrayal of a Roman soldier's combat dress you will notice right away the tall helmets with extended bright red plumage, combined with an elongated shield, creating the impression at a distance the soldier is seven feet tall and invincible! The soldier's also carried imposing looking weapons, once again to give the impression of larger size and ability. Even the troop formations themselves gave the illusion at a distance of more men than were actually present, making the army as a whole seem larger and more formidable.

Find ways to let your consumers, as well as your competition know immediately and in a big way that you are not only *in* business, but *doing* business as well. And remember, despite the hype, they still didn't build Rome in a day.

3. **Establish: In other words…dig in! Before you can begin conquering and defending your newly acquired empire, you must first "establish" a base of operations from which to attack outward. The best base to progress forward from is your first few sales. Get those under your belt as fast as possible, if for nothing more than psychological reasons.**

I will assume that your initial entry into the market was sufficient enough to gain some amount of sales, if not actual market share itself. After you have gotten your feet wet with those first few sales and have a working knowledge of what it takes to sell in that particular market, you must compile a list of what you have and what you will need to begin turning those first few sales into actual market share. Entrench yourself around *existing* market share. Defend it from those who wish to take it from you and then you are ready to begin expanding on that foundation.

There are two ways to deal with any problems or adverse conditions you may encounter in your market. You can have a plan to get out of trouble, or you can have a plan to avoid it in the first place. I suggest the latter. This relates directly to the concept of *choosing your battles*. Too many sales organizations literally go broke trying to enter and defend markets they shouldn't even have been in in the first place.

You may be able to capture the flag on top of the hill, but at what cost? Will your efforts and resources be more successful and/or profitable directed at another market? These are considerations that must be made before dedicating time, resources, or effort to establish yourself in a market that can't or won't yield the results necessary to warrant the time, resources, or effort. One plus one may equal two, but that does you no good if the answer you need three.

I've seen individuals enter a market place, make a powerful impact, become well established quickly, maintain an effective defense while aggressively expanding existing market share, and still fail because there was not enough of that market share to sustain their long-term objectives. If you need anywhere near 100 percent market share to reach your goals, change your goals or find a new market.

4. **Conquer: Seize the high ground by first planning the shortest route to it. Only defenders benefit from a prolonged attack. There is a difference between conquering the competition and conquering the market. You have conquered your market when you can consistently achieve your production goals for that market, regardless of what the competition is doing. You have conquered your competition when you reach a consistent level of production the competition is unable or unwilling to challenge successfully. Again, neither requires 100 percent, just a sufficient percentage to accomplish your goals. That percentage is what you'll be defending.**

5. **Defend: Once you have entered the market and begun to establish yourself there, you must then have a plan to defend that which you have established. The competition might not know or care that you *entered* the race, but once you begin to establish yourself in it, they must take an interest, if not actual measures to deal with you.**

The best place to begin defending what you have is to establish an effective quality service program directed at those clients and market share you have already gained. Since existing market share is so crucial to any future marketing plans, that's where the competition will likely attack first—your existing market share. Do not fall into the all too common business mentality of being so focused on conquering distant shores that you forget about the home front.

I go into greater detail later about the creation and implementation of an effective quality service program. But for now, I want you to start thinking about a few things. Are there any ways you can be of even *more* service to your clients? What programs are you currently utilizing that deal directly with keeping satisfied customers, satisfied? Do you have any ideas regarding how to improve upon your level of service that you would like to try? Good, because that's where we're going to start in the chapter on "Quality Service."

6. **Expand: This is the goal of every business! Why? Because when it comes to success and achieving our goals, enough is *never* enough—especially true when it comes to market share. A business or business person that is not constantly in a state of moving forward is moving backward, even if he remains where they are, because the competition, your customers, and the market are never standing still.**

We discussed earlier that there are basically two types of markets, g*eographic* and *demographic*. Now let me tell you about another even more important market place—the consumers *mind*. That is your *real* battleground. It is where your battle to conquer your market will be won or lost. Win their hearts and minds, and you'll win their business. Here are some tips:

1. **Price is almost always a deciding factor. Beating the competition in price may be enough.**

2. **Promote superior service as much as superior quality or price. Many consumers will gladly pay more money for more and better service.**

3. **Offer a superior product if possible.**

4. **Constantly seek new or different products to gain the attention of existing clients.**

5. **Fast delivery is crucial; consumers want it** *yesterday*.

6. **Use more appealing packaging or promotion. Surveys and market data will help.**

7. **Make your product easy to buy.**

8. **Distinguish yourself from your competition not only by appearing different, but also better. This includes efforts to educate those consumers as to why** *your* **different is better. They may not understand that new is improved unless the customers are taught otherwise. So who's going to teach them if you don't? The more they know, the more you grow.**

"He who wishes to secure the good of others, has already secured his own."

CONFUCIUS

CHAPTER 13: THE CUSTOMER

$

"Right or wrong, the customer is always right."
MARSHALL FIELD

Today's salespeople are dealing with the most sophisticated consumers in human history—and those consumers know it! Thanks to the Internet and modern communications, sales professionals literally have access to the whole world as their market place. However, it'll take *more* than just a better mousetrap for that world to beat a path to your door.

Access to information is access to opportunity. And as luck would have it, we are living in the *information* (opportunity) age. What once took entire organizations days, if not weeks to accomplish just a few short years ago, can now be done in a matter of minutes by an individual. Entire markets that were once beyond your reach are now at your fingertips. There has never been a time in the history of civilization that offered consumers more goods and services or made them easier to locate and purchase.

Here's the downside of this new and opportunistic environment. Many sales professionals and organizations are not *taking advantage of their advantage.*

Thanks to all these new means of communication and networking, sales professionals have never been so close to their consumers—*or so far away.* All too often, sales organizations use modern communication methods designed and implemented to allow consumers more access and convenience, as a firewall or barrier between themselves and those very consumers. *Please press one, then the pound sign....*

When gadgets can do the job of a salesperson, there will be no more jobs for salespeople to do—except to sell the gadgets.

Many purchases today are a result of what's called "impulse buying." All of these gadgets of convenience have made it easier and faster for buyers to locate and purchase what they need when they need it, and consumers have adapted and responded to this new environment in ever-increasing numbers.

Dead weight can cost as much as live weight. Don't let your selling system be nothing more than a fancy coffin.

I mentioned at the opening of this chapter that salespeople today are dealing with the most sophisticated and informed consumers in history. And we discussed how those sophisticated and informed consumers buy what they buy based just as much on emotion as they do on logic. As a result, we have smart and informed buyers who will buy right then and there (impulse buying), if their "emotions" or "logic" direct them to.

Keep in mind that any consumer related technology or systems you employ should benefit the customer as much, if not more than the company utilizing it. Unfortunately, too many *customer service* based organizations use technology to service *themselves* more than their clients.

Any system that makes it easier for you to sell while at the same time making it harder for your customers to buy is not a fair-value trade off. Trust me; that system will end up costing you a lot more money than you originally paid for it. For example, those automated phone systems with a hold feature are common and fairly inexpensive, and yet they may be costing those companies a fortune—given the fact that 50 percent of callers placed on hold for more than two minutes will simply hang up. Many of those pleasant hold music tracks have cost those companies more money than they would have paid to hire AC/DC to play live.

Technology should always be used in addition to, not instead of, personal contact.

You stay *up* with the competition by serving the needs of your customers. You stay *ahead* of the competition by *anticipating* those needs. It's the only way you can position yourself *ahead* of your competition—by getting to the customer *first*. Therefore, before you begin serving the needs of your clients, you must first develop a plan to anticipate those needs, then position yourself accordingly in the sales chain.

The first place to start better serving the needs of your customers is at the source—you. *You* are the first link in the sales chain; therefore, you should be the *closest* link to your clients. Even if you are not the first link in your particular sales chain, you are still the most *important* link. If you don't serve your customers the way they demand and deserved to be served, you may end up the *missing* link.

The first thing before determining *where* to look for customers is determining *who* your customers are in sufficient numbers to comprise a market. I will assume that if your business is selling surfboards you're not sending catalogs to Wyoming. I'm also going to assume that you have some idea of who your potential customers are and generally where they can be found. For some salespeople, it's anyone with a pulse and five bucks. But if the requirements exceed that, there will probably be some sort of selling *relationship* between you and your consumers. Even if you never come into direct contact with them, the closer that relationship is, the more profitable it's going to be.

I can spend the rest of this book and ten more like it trying to teach you the importance and application of a successful buyer/seller relationship.

So let me condense it into three simple words— *folks are folks.* The same things you may like or dislike about your product or service are probably the very same things your customers do as well. An approach that appeals to you may be just as effective with your clients…or not! The only way to know what the likes and dislikes of your customers are is to know your customers. A good way to begin knowing them is by knowing *yourself.* Are you selling something *you* would buy?

I have found that the best way to *serve* the customer is to *care* about the customer. If you sincerely care about the people you are serving, even if you do not know them personally, that care and concern for them and their interests will have a direct effect on your productivity. The better you serve them, the more they will want to be served by you. Once again, put the customer first and you'll never come in second.

The motto of my company Phil Kreider, Inc. is, "A *Cause! Not a Corporation*," meaning, it's not just what we do, but how and why we do it. Do you as an individual or as a business have a mission statement, or a philosophy, or at least a slogan that reflects your commitment to your customers? Whether it's as simple as a company motto or as complex as an entire quality service program, it must reflect your positive and appreciative attitude toward those you serve.

Consumers can be as unpredictable as the weather. Their likes and dislikes can, and often do, change literally overnight. Despite the fact they are constantly distracted by the never ending introduction of newer and better products, one constant always remains the same—how they expect you to treat them in exchange for their business.

It seems the art of selling to today's consumers, in some cases, has been reduced to a mathematical equation of sorts. Advertisers now know which colors, which words, and which images will induce the customer to buy their product over another, or even to make the purchase at all. But that's only half the battle. The other half is still, and always will be, *the salesperson*. That is why coffee *shops* do more business than coffee *machines*. That's also why "press one to speak to a live operator" is still chosen by callers ten times more often than any other option. Coffee machines aside, we are still human beings that seek out and appreciate interaction with other human beings. A personal touch still carries the ultimate weight with today's consumers, despite the ease and convenience of automated selling and purchasing systems.

Today's consumer, just like yesterday's consumer, and I'm sure like tomorrow's consumer, will always want that personal touch. They want to look into your eyes when they hand over their money and see in your eyes that they've made the right decision. A machine can make money, but it can seldom make a *sale*. Besides, in every science fiction movie ever made, the machines are always evil!

> *"Treat every customer as if your world revolves around them…it does.."*

UNKNOWN

CHAPTER 14: THE COMPETITION

A Tribute to My Competitors

"My competitors do more for me than my friends. My friends are too polite to point out my weaknesses, but my competitors go to great expense to boldly advertise them. My competitors are attentive, hard working and would take my business away from me if they could. They keep me alert and inspire me to find ways to improve my products and services. If I had no competitors...I would be less efficient and inattentive. I can use the discipline they force upon me. I salute my competitors. They have been good for me. God bless them all!"

What type of person would view a competitor as a friend? Only a salesperson!

As a former public speaker, I had the opportunity to do a lot of traveling around the country, which involved an extensive amount of air travel. I remember on one particular flight I was reading a golf magazine that ranked the top one hundred professional golfers by score and earnings. I noticed that the difference between the top golfer's and the one-hundredth golfer's score was less than a few strokes. But here's the amazing part—the difference in their *earnings* was millions of dollars! Proving that in golf, like sales, you don't need to decimate or even dominate the competition to end up on top. Even the smallest margin of victory can pay big results.

Speaking of golf, I believe the same principles apply to the game of sales. You are constantly competing against the other players (your competition). You are constantly competing against the course itself (your market). Clubs matter too (your product or service). That would make your customers the ball. Your job is to use your clubs, combined with your knowledge about the course, and the skills you have developed, to drive the ball (customer) to the hole (sale). The good news is it only takes a single stroke to beat the competition.

Another thing you are always competing against is *time*, or in some cases, *timing*. For example, who invented the telephone, Alexander Graham Bell or Elija Gray? The answer: They *both* did. But unfortunately for Gray, Bell made it to the patents office four hours before he did, which is why there are no schools named after Gray. If there is a customer right now that wants to buy your particular product or service, all you may need to do is get there ahead of your competitors. Without adding anything else, changing the "timing" of what you are already doing to locate clients may be one of the best things you can do to increase your production immediately.

I know that realtors understand the importance of timing when it comes to prospecting for clients. That's why they always call at dinnertime. It's the "prime hour" for people to be home. The same amount of prospecting calls made during the afternoon, when most people are *not* home, yield only a fraction of the results the exact same amount of calls made after 5:00 p.m. do. It may take an extra few seconds to apologize for interrupting their meal, but a small price to pay for increasing your income by 400 percent, literally overnight.

You have a few options when it comes to dealing with your competitors. Number one, you can ignore them and hope they go away. Number two, you can deal with them. Or number three, you can wait for them to *deal with you*. I know from personal experience that number one seldom ever works, so in reality you have only two options.

Believe it or not, there are *positive* influences healthy competition can have. But let's not break out the love-beads just yet. There's nothing those "positive influences" would love to do more than to attend your going out of business sale. That is why the rest of this chapter is going to deal with you being a *less than positive* influence on your competition.

For every *action* against your competition there is probably going to be some form of *reaction* from them, and hopefully vice-versa. If not, remember, any market *not* worth defending may not be worth attacking in the first place. But if there is competition there to begin with, I suppose there's going to be business there as well. Any marketing plan that you are considering directing toward the competition should also include for the competition's response to your actions. Most businesses with hard earned market share are just as tenacious when it comes to defending it as they were in getting it in the first place. My guess is they already have a plan in place for dealing with *upstarts* like you.

The first step once you have identified a potential market is to conduct a *competitor analysis* of every competition source within that market. Don't worry about attack plans yet. Just find out who your competition is, what they have going *for* them, and what they have going *against* them. Your plan of attack will be based on those three factors.

Don't automatically discount some of the smaller fish in your pond. Salespeople with the smallest market share tend to fight the hardest to keep what little they have. It's easier to dodge a charging elephant than it is a bullet.

Make your competitor evaluation as detailed and inclusive as possible. The bulk of your attack campaign will be based on that information. Each strategy will be determined by not only *your* strengths and weaknesses but your competitors as well. To paraphrase, keep your customers close, and your competitors *closer*.

Taking care of your customers is the best defense against your competition *taking care of you*.

You must determine where your competition is currently at in relation to the market so that you can accurately plot a course to get ahead of them. The first step to *maintaining* the lead is to first *gain* the lead. That's always the prime objective.

Here are some basic strategies when dealing with the competition:

1. **The best way to knock the competition is to *not* knock the competition. However, you must be knowledgeable enough about your competitors and their offerings to articulate those differences or answer any questions the customer may have regarding you versus them. Point out any misconceptions the consumer might have about your competitor's product or service, especially *false* beliefs regarding superiority or price. The bottom line is this; if you do not believe your product has at least *some* advantage over the competition, then maybe the grass *is* a little greener on the other side of the fence. Sometimes it makes more sense to switch than fight. Don't ever be afraid to mention or discuss the competition. Just don't make tearing down the competition part of the building up and selling of you.**

2. **Divide and conquer, and** *keep* **dividing and conquering. Taking competitors on piece-meal one at a time is the best way to avoid giving them a reason or an opportunity to rally together for a successful defense or even counter attack. I've seen organizations take so long to enter into and establish a** *beachhead* **in certain markets that the competition had plenty of time and opportunity to identify the threat, develop a successful defense, and then aggressively counter attack. I've also seen salespeople enter a market in such a way that their competition had no choice but to band together for defense—Walmart comes to mind. Remember what I said earlier, 80 percent of your resources and effort when entering any new market must be directed at the initial phase of entry.**

3. **There is strength in numbers—especially number one! If, currently, you are** *not* **number one in your respective market, then at least you have a goal to work toward. The obvious advantage to being number one is that it's always easier to hold the high ground than it is to seize it in the first place. The last thing you want to be doing as a salesperson is playing offense all the time. In the beginning it is fine, just remember your goal is to seize the high ground so you can then spend a lot less effort and resources holding it, while your competitors have to increase their efforts and resources trying to take it back. Adding to your own pile while depleting the opponents—**that's **the advantage of being on top.**

4. **Be an honorable and gracious opponent. In other words, not only avoid burning your own bridges, but other people's bridges as well—if for no other reason**

than today's competitors may be tomorrow's co-workers. Ninety percent of all the sales professionals I have ever managed either came from, or went to, a competitor at some point in our relationship.

The best way for you to take care of your competition is for you to take care of your customers. That means the only competitor that can really defeat you is...you. Either way, the job will get done by someone. If you don't take care of your customers, someone else will.

"I start where the last man left off."

THOMAS A. EDISON

CHAPTER 15: EDUCATION AND TRAINING

"Education costs money, but then so does ignorance."

There is only one way to begin this chapter, and that is to congratulate you for making it this far. When it comes to education and self improvement, the first thing most of us look for is a short cut or an emergency exit. Reading this book, I am going to assume, is no different. Once again, congratulations for making it this far.

You may know exactly what you want in life, but do you know exactly how you're going to get it? If not, there's no time like the present to start.

Remember what I said earlier, awareness is the first step to education and education is the first step to change and growth. Knowing what you want is a great first step. You'd be surprised how many people go through their entire lives not only never working toward their goals, but also never having any goals to work toward in the first place. Education is learning how to make your dreams come true. So, unless you have a genie or fairy godmother to do that for you, keep reading.

Unfortunately, many of us never seem to get past the awareness stage. Awareness is crucial, but knowledge without application is worse than useless. The first place to begin changing your life and circumstances is with education, which unfortunately is the *last* place most people start.

Why do you suppose I began this chapter by congratulating you on making it this far in the book? Wasn't it a *given* that since you purchased the book you would naturally read it? What good is paying for something that you don't intend to use? Do you think that everyone who purchased and began reading this book has made it to this point? Or for that matter, even began reading it at all? If your answer was *yes*, think again. Let me share with you a true story.

A few years ago, I was the keynote speaker at a sales convention on Long Island, New York. The topic was personal marketing. As any speaker will tell you, although we do get paid quite well for a speaking engagement, the real profits come from what's called B.O.R.s (back of the room product sales). Those back of the room sales alone can often bring a speaker two or three times their original speaking fee.

As usual, my staff brought with us a large quantity of topic related materials to be sold at the convention to the attendees. One item was a four CD program on personal marketing.

The first day of the convention, we sold over one hundred of those programs at $40 each. That evening, when I returned to my hotel room, there was an urgent message from my production manager back in Los Angeles telling me to call him immediately. When I got him on the phone he said, "Whatever you do, don't sell any of the personal marketing programs!" It seems that through a production error, CD number three was completely blank. I then told him, "No problem...except one," the fact that we had just sold over one hundred of the programs that afternoon.

There was only one solution. Immediately manufacture an additional one hundred plus copies of CD three and have them ready to be mailed out with a letter of apology when those one hundred plus individuals who purchased the program called our office to complain. It's been several years since we sold those blank CDs, and as of today, we have received less than twenty-five requests for a replacement CD. Do you know what that means? It means that 75 percent of those who paid $40 for a program that I have no doubt could have helped their careers immensely, never even made it to the third CD! I'll bet you that $40 that every one of those programs is still sitting on a shelf somewhere, no doubt collecting dust alongside all the other wasted opportunities of that salesperson's career. The individual who can read (or in this case listen) and *does not*, is no better off than the individual who *cannot*.

Now do you see why congratulations were in order? And not because we are well past chapter three, but because you kept your commitment. Remember back in chapter one, I challenged you to complete this program to the best of your ability, then to implement what you learned. Well, you are one third of the way there. Keep going!

What converts knowledge into success? *Application*. It's actually using the tools you spent your time, money, and effort acquiring. How many great sales techniques have you learned over the years that you were certain would raise your production, but for some reason you never implemented or even thought about since you first learned them? Tools only work when they're working.

There's one pitfall when it comes to education. *We don't know what we don't know*. So how do we go about learning what we don't even know exists? A crucial part of the education process is to first develop an awareness and understanding of your current level of knowledge and education. For instance, a sixth grader would not try to immediately jump to the twelfth grade, unless they were under the *mistaken impression* they were an eleventh grader. That's the importance of having an honest and accurate understanding of where you currently are and where you are *not*...at least not yet. You need to know your current location before you can effectively plot a course to your destination.

They say that a little knowledge can be a dangerous thing. Well, so can *too much* knowledge. Whenever I began a new training program, the first thing I would do is separate the class into two groups. I'd place all the new salespeople in one group and all the experienced *old pro's* in the second group—hopefully as far away as possible from the first group. Here's why; only one group knew enough to know they didn't know enough, so at least they were open to learning it from me. Guess which group that was.

There are two major areas where education can immediately improve your career. One is the acquisition of knowledge. The other is development of skill. Knowledge is what you *know*. Skill is how you *use* what you know. I consider myself a trainer above all else—and I believe a pretty good one—but no matter how capable an instructor I am, or how able my students, *skill cannot be learned in a classroom* any more than playing golf can be learned from a book. You can learn what to do from a book or in a classroom, but you can't learn *how* to do it—not in the real sense of the word...only in theory, not application. Would you rather be successful for real, or just in theory?

What's the fastest way for any salesperson to develop people skills? STP (See the People). Yep, face to face, belly to belly—you can't learn combat techniques from your foxhole.

I consider education not only the accumulation of knowledge and skill but also of resources, especially resources that help develop our skill and increase our knowledge. That's the difference between education and training. Education is what we *learn* and training is what we're *taught*.

I feel that one of the characteristics of a true sales professional is his awareness that he must *learn* more, to *do* more. If you're one of those salespeople who regularly seek out and participate in educational opportunities, I think that speaks volumes about you and your approach to this profession. As a recruiter for sales organizations, I always recruited my best salespeople from classrooms, not sales offices.

Anyone who has ever managed a sales organization understands that education and training are just as valuable a commodity to any sales staff as the products or services they sell. In my opinion, the most important member of the sales team is the sales trainer. If your organization has a designated sales trainer I suggest you meet with them and at least find out all the resources and information they have available. If you want to be the number one salesperson in your office or organization, spend the next six months learning everything the trainer knows. In fact, it's their job to make sure you do exactly that.

Here's a frightening thought; studies show that the average American reads only one book per year, while over 50 percent of the population reports watching *Wheel of Fortune* on a regular basis.

The easiest person in the world to sell something to is a salesperson! Which means your training library should be filled to the brim with training materials (sold to you or otherwise)…right?

If you want to *earn* more, then you have to *learn* more. It stands to reason that the best way to earn more money for your time is to make yourself and your time more valuable. Education is how you do that. Your educational and self-improvement library should cost more than your wardrobe.

Complacency is a career killer. I always said that the absolute worst thing that can happen to any new salesperson is to have easy success at the beginning of his career. Every time I saw a shooting star suddenly and dramatically rise in a sales organization, I usually saw him crash back to earth before long. That early success probably convinced him this job was going to be easy. So he just sat back and waited for the rest of his money just to come walking through the door. But more often than not, it was that same salesperson who ended up walking *out* the door (for good) long before that easy money came walking in.

> *"I hear and I forget; I see and I*
> *remember; I do and I understand."*
>
> CHINESE PROVERB

CHAPTER 16: MENTORS AND MODELS

"A candle loses nothing by lighting another candle."   ERIN MAJORS

I f you take the time and effort to look for them, you'll discover there are countless individuals in just about every field who are not only ready and able, but *willing* to generously share their knowledge and wisdom with others who take an interest in and appreciate such an opportunity. Many of history's most successful people directly attribute their success to the leadership and guidance of others. I'm sure there are certain individuals you have encountered who have helped shape your life or career for the better.

Whether we realize it or not, many of the actions we regularly engage in are for the approval or acceptance of those whose opinion or favorable response we value or seek.

We all have a need to be accepted, liked, or at least acknowledged by those we respect or admire. This explains the popularity of gangs, cults, and other unhealthy associations. We will dress, behave, achieve, and basically do whatever it takes to be accepted by those whose acceptance we seek. That inner desire can prove a valuable asset if you can effectively harness and direct it. If you choose positive role models and mentors who inspire within you superior or positive performance, you can use those individuals as booster rockets, so to speak, to get yourself to the next level in your life and your career.

If there is a group within the office whose primary activities include non-business or socializing activities, you may wish to avoid them altogether. You may wish to do the same with the associations in your personal life as well. Water has a way of seeking its own level. Be careful not to become guilty of failure by association. Eagles don't hang out in duck ponds.

President Woodrow Wilson once said, *"Not only use all the brains you have, but all the brains you can borrow as well."*

For some reason many of us will often work harder to live up to the expectations of other's than we will to live up to our own. Sometimes we simply try harder because we know someone is watching. Not only will we work harder to live *up* to the expectations of others, we can also work just as hard to live *down* to them. For instance, studies have shown that when a parent continually tells a child that he or she has a deficiency, you can bet that child is going to live up to, or in this case down to, the expectations of someone the child would normally look to for guidance and support. An effective mentor knows the value of encouragement.

Effective mentors also have an eye for talent. They can usually spot capabilities in us long before we see them ourselves. And a good mentor is always looking for that next diamond in the rough. Be sure to keep your eyes *open* for those higher-ups keeping an eye *out* for someone like you.

One common trait among the mentors that I've had over the years is that they were not only someone that *I* looked up to, but they were also admired by just about everyone else in the office/organization. If I admired someone that no one else did, I had to take a closer look at my assessment of the individual. What was I missing that everyone else saw, or what did I see that others didn't?

You'll need several models and mentors to assist in your development over the course of your career. The most effective mentor in the world still cannot *be all things to all people*. Each mentor will have one or two primary characteristics that resemble what you would like to develop for yourself. Each will have their area of expertise or some defining accomplishment that you wish duplicate for yourself. They will act as your guide to help lead you to where they already are. Mentors are already familiar with the path you seek to travel as well as the short cuts and pitfalls along the way.

You'd be surprised how much time and headache an effective mentor can save you with just a short meeting once a week—perhaps over lunch. Just be sure to pick up the check...and leave a big tip. Remember the mentors motto; *what goes around, comes around*. If you pay for the mentor's lunch and leave the server a large tip, you show your mentor that you are someone who appreciates and values the time and effort of others.

You know or work with an individual whose style of dress you admire. He may project an image that you would to like present. This person may be a total failure in almost every other aspect of his life, but at least he always looked sharp. You may wish to designate that person as your *fashion mentor* so to speak. Start by building your wardrobe similar to the style and fashion of the person's you admire. If you compliment him on a particular outfit, also inquire as to where he purchased it. Find out where he shops and do the same.

It is also important that the models and mentors you choose have some personal contact with your life. An effective mentor really needs to be someone you can meet with and receive direct guidance from.

I mentioned in the previous chapter that *many are willing to learn but few are willing to be taught*. The first step to be "taught" is putting your ego aside and admit there is someone who is better at something right now than you are. It's not that they are better than you as a person; it's just that they are better at *doing* something. If you can't find anyone who is better at something than you are, put down this book right now and go save the planet!

First, identify what the potential mentor is better at, then exactly what it is that makes him better at it. Remember, it's not *who* he is, it's *what* he does. Just make sure you can do what he is doing. I admire and respect Tom Brady's playing ability, but no matter how much he mentored me, he could never get me to the point where I could be the quarterback of the New England Patriots.

The best way to repay good advice is by *acting* on it.

Important note: Don't let your eagerness to be a *mentee* become a burden to your *mentor*, unless he's expressed an interest in becoming a foster parent. If he does indeed meet the basic criteria of being more successful at something than you are, chances are he is also busy maintaining that level of success, with perhaps less time to answer questions than you have to ask them. If possible, try to compile a *team* of models and mentors.

The best tribute you can pay to your own mentors is to one day become someone else's.

> **"It is true. I have reached higher than most, but only because I have stood upon the shoulders of giants."**
>
> ALBERT EINSTEIN

SECTION 4: The Art of Selling

"The road to service is traveled with integrity, compassion and understanding. People don't care how much you know until they know how much you care."

CHAPTER 17: EFFECTIVE COMMUNICATION

"What you do speaks so loudly I can't hear what you're saying."   R.W. Emerson

The ability to speak to others does not make someone an effective communicator. An effective communicator is able to create enthusiasm and confidence with his words to the point of motivating the listener to act, while at the same time managing expectations.

The brain is a remarkable thing. It starts working the minute we are born and doesn't stop until we start talking. Every day opportunities for salespeople are won and lost by nothing more than the words that come out of their mouths.

When it comes to selling, *talking the talk* is just as important as *walking the walk*.

As a salesperson, you don't need to convince everyone you meet that it's *love at first sight.* Just get them to remember who you are, what you sell, and where they can find you when they're ready to buy. An eight-year-old with a lemonade stand can accomplish this with a cardboard sign...usually with misspelled words!

Effective communication involves more than just what you say. Believe it or not, that's the *least* important aspect of communication. When it comes to conveying your entire message and establishing trust and credibility, *how* you say it is even more important than *what* you say. Effective communication involves *body* language not just *verbal* language.

Whenever we are physically speaking to someone, the content of our message gets broken down into three distinct parts. The first part is *what* you say; the actual words you use account for approximately 7 percent of the message your listener is receiving. The second part is your vocal conveyance; *how* you say the words account for approximately 38 percent of the message your listener is receiving. A whopping *57 percent* of your message is conveyed visually or physically. As far as your listener is concerned, *how* you say something is twice as important as *what* you actually say.

Twenty-five percent of the people you meet will judge you entirely by your appearance. An additional 50 percent will judge you *in part* by your appearance. That means 75 percent of the people you come into direct contact with will make a judgment about you and your message before you even open your mouth!

Not only is your body language and physical appearance primary determining factors in whether or not your message is being properly *sent*. The body language of the listener is a prime indicator of whether or not your message is being properly *received*. An effective communicator is not only effective at *sending* communication signals, but also at *receiving* them as well. Effective communication is always a two-way street. Turn it into a one-way street and you'll soon find yourself on a dead end.

When it comes to effective communication, the key is *confidence*. The message is diminished whenever the receiver has a lack of confidence in the message or the messenger. The best way to get others to have confidence in you and your message is for you to have confidence in those things yourself.

Credibility Damaging Factors

1. **Rigidity: Lack of animation and gestures**

2. **Nervousness: Fidgeting or over-animation**

3. **Voice: Too fast, too high, monotone**

4. **Eyes: Avoiding eye contact, eye dart**

5. **Facials: Pursed lips, poker face**

6. **Hands: Sweaty palms, limp handshake**

7. **Vocals: Non-words, stuttering**

8. **Mouth: Covering with hand when speaking**

9. **Hair: Playing with, running fingers through**

10. **Head: Nodding or shaking too fast**

11. **Visuals: Unprofessional appearance; visuals too complicated or misleading**

If you find yourself speaking in a public or professional atmosphere, your appearance and manner of dress will play a vital role in not only *your* credibility, but also the credibility of your message as well. Your projected appearance and image becomes paramount in your ability to get your audience to *act* on your message.

As a public speaker on tour, I would often stand in the back of the room and observe the audience as well as the preceding speakers. Undoubtedly, someone whom I'd never met before would approach me and ask if I was the speaker. I would say, yes, and ask him how he knew. The truth is I didn't have to ask. From past experience, I knew exactly how he knew—by the way I was dressed.

Here are some tips for utilizing your appearance and image as a positive force when communicating and not a credibility damaging one.

Communicator Appearance
1. **Properly fitting suit or outfit**

2. **No excessive jewelry**

3. **A quality watch**

4. **Buttons buttoned, none missing**

5. **Shoes shined**

6. **Unbitten, clean, and trimmed, finger nails**

7. **Head and facial hair neatly combed and trimmed**

8. **Clean, pressed, coordinated clothing**

Another important dynamic of effective communication is body language. Both the sending and interpreting of body language can be an excellent communication tool in not only conscious but also subconscious messages. Can you imagine that? Being able to control how someone feels toward you or the way he receives your message simply by the physical actions associated with delivering your message. The truly effective leaders and communicators, as well as the most successful advertisers, use this on us all the time.

When it comes to communication in the field of selling, the salesperson is often faced with the difficult task of getting the prospect from a negative or indifferent frame of mind to a receptive one in a very short amount of time. Your words as well as your actions must be properly *displayed* if they are to build the necessary rapport and establish that the prospect is effectively receiving the message.

Since you never get a second chance to make a first impression, and since 75 percent of the people you talk to will form an opinion of you based entirely on physical appearance, and 97 percent of what you say is received based on *how* you say it, I think a few minor adjustments to your sales pitch may have a dramatic effect on your success rate. Now let's find out exactly how to *walk the walk* as well *talk the talk*.

There are two ways that body language is effectively used in the art of communication. One way is by *following* or mirroring the actions of the listener. The second way is by *leading* the listener into following your actions...all the way to the dotted line.

When I refer to *mirroring*, I do not mean literally, although in a way, I do. The trick is to duplicate the actions of the listener as closely as possible without them becoming aware of what you are actually doing. Accomplishing that is even easier than it sounds.

When I conduct my communicating and negotiating workshops, the *mirroring* or *following* exercises seem to give the students the most trouble. The students assume during the exercise that the listener is actually *listening* to what the speakers are saying or paying attention to what they're doing. Nothing could be further from the truth. I go to the extent of beginning the workshop by videotaping an on-stage interview with several students. I will choose an unrelated topic and sit there with them for several minutes asking them questions and interacting with them. Duplicating every move they make during the entire demonstration. In the mirroring portion of the program, I show the class the video, asking them to pay attention to *my* body language. At this point, it's very obvious, almost to the point of being comical, that the whole time during the actual interview, neither the students *nor the audience* were even remotely aware of what I was doing. Believe me; when mirroring is done properly, the listener won't notice—they never do.

The *"following"* technique is used to set up the *"leading"* technique, where the listener begins to duplicate *your* actions subconsciously. I know that must sound strange, but after a period of effective mirroring, the prospect will subconsciously begin to mirror you! That is when you know the mirroring process has worked. Once the prospect begins to *follow* your lead, sufficient rapport has been established and you now have an open door to your message. No sale is made until proper rapport with the client has been established.

Another necessary part of the physical and visual communication process is the ability to interpret the visual and physical communication signals of the receiver or listener. How they listen is just as important as how they respond. When you know how to properly identify and interpret the communication signals the client is sending you (two-way street), then you can adjust your message and body language accordingly. This will put you in the situation of directing the prospect's actions as opposed to merely reacting to them, which is the essence of selling.

Body Language Interpretation

1. **Silence: Message not understood or received**

2. **Client stands up: He is finished listening**

3. **Furrows brow: He is curious or even worse, skeptical**

4. **Clasping hands above head: Doubts believability of message**

5. **Arms or legs crossed: Tense, uncomfortable, or isolating himself**

6. **Rub nose: Puzzlement**

7. **Rubbing chin: Evaluating information**

8. **Lean back in chair: Indifference to, or disdain for, the message**

9. **Frown: Displeasure**

10. **Rapid blinking: Low concentration**

11. **Finger tapping: Impatience and/or agitation**

12. **Nod head: Approval**

13. Clear throat: Nervous or anxious

14. Steeple fingers: Superiority and confidence

15. Looking at watch: Boredom or impatience

Naturally, there are countless other ways a person can communicate visual and physical signals. The higher your level of awareness regarding those signals, the greater your ability to detect, interpret, and effectively respond to those signals. So pay attention to what the listener is telling you while you're telling them.

And practice—lots and lots of practice. You can begin these exercises immediately on those around you right now. Begin by looking for some of the body language signals I just described. Practice mirroring during the next conversation you have with someone. If that proves effective, proceed to practicing leading, and rapport building. Once you get the hang of it, you will see changes in the way those around you respond to you. After a while, it even gets fun playing *lead the follower*.

When it comes to those you will be effectively communicating with, there are basically three types of receivers—audio, visual, and kinesthetic. The main focus of the audio type personality would be on what is *said* or the actual message itself. Someone who is more visually oriented would focus mainly on what he *sees*, and a kinesthetic type would be focused on what he can *touch*. When it comes to an effective sales presentation or marketing medium, it is important to incorporate within your message parts that appeal directly to each of the three different types of receivers. I would target all three types with every message due to the fact you never know which type you are communicating with at the time.

An effective sales presentation would include a strong and credible message, delivered by an effective communicator, including visual and physical aspects that get the receiver involved and enthusiastic enough to act upon the message. Regardless of the medium, quality of the sender's message, or the personality type of the receiver, the ultimate goal is to make you and your message something the client can relate to, wants to hear, and believes in.

Any teacher will tell you that students retain 70 percent more of what they're taught when a visual aid is used in the lesson. If want your message to worth retaining then I strongly suggest you make it *visually* appealing and memorable.

Later in the book, I have included an entire chapter on the art of negotiation. What you learn from *this* chapter will be directly related to what we discuss in the chapter on negotiating. So I hope you have been paying attention. It is impossible to separate communication and negotiation. They both go hand in hand. Communication is basically a form of conveying a message. Negotiation is communicating a message to achieve an objective. We use communication to negotiate and get what we want.

One of the best ways to use communication as a rapport building tool, whether it be a personal or business conversation, is to use the person's name… and use it often. Face it; if there is one word that gets and keeps your attention more than any other word it's your name—or maybe the word "fire!"

There are basically two types of conversations in which the average person engages—*formal* and *Informal*. Formal communication is usually done in a business or non-personal environment. During personal/informal conversations, it almost seems we become a different person as we easily and effectively communicate to others in a relaxed and confident manner. With a little bit of practice those formal conversations can become as easy and comfortable as the informal. When you can talk to your customers in the same relaxed and confident manner that you do your friends and family you will truly have achieved the level of master sales professional.

Although, after a while, your formal and professional conversations can be delivered with the ease and comfort of your personal ones, I would advise not using the exact same manner and style for both; business is still business if you know what I mean. There is such a thing as being *too personal* in certain business situations. But overall, it seems the intimate and personal communications we have with those we feel comfortable with are more effective simply because of the relaxed nature of the communicator.

If you can learn to have the same natural confidence, sincerity, and comfort in your formal, business communications as you do in your personal ones, then eventually the same level of likeability and believability will be present in both. The true master of communication is able to talk to everyone as though they were personal lifelong friends.

Just like effective friendships, effective communication is a two-way street. In order to be a truly effective communicator, you must know how to *send* as well as *receive* dialogue. Communication between two individuals is nothing more than the exchange of information. You can convey information and receive information at the same time. This is known as the L C & C or *Information Exchange Process*.

Listen: There are two ways to listen, passive and active. Children and house pets specialize in the first one. Passive is more *hearing* than listening. Active listening is the secret to mastering the negotiation and communication process. To actively listen is to hear, absorb, understand, and formulate responses to what the other party is saying. Yogi Berra once said, "You can hear a lot by listening."

Clarify: Active listening means involvement in the communication process. Expanding on what you hear to get more information. It may be necessary to clarify what the sender has told you in order to evaluate the message accurately. If necessary, ask follow up or expanding questions so that you fully understand the entire message and its context. Paraphrasing what a person has just said is a great way not only to clarify what has been said but also to let the sender know you are actively listening.

Consult: That means take an *active* role in the conversation. Think *team* concept. Use a lot of *we, us,* and *our* verbiage whenever possible. This will let the other party know that you care, understand, and are on *their* side.

Effective communication involves delivering all the information necessary to get your idea or message across to the intended receiver. Just because *you* understand, don't assume they do as well.

Here are two separate, but related facts. Imagine the first half of this message without the second half. "I have to put the cat out." Pause here and think about the partial message I just conveyed. Do you think you understood fully what I said? Now here is the rest of my message: "Do you have a fire extinguisher?" Do you see how only a portion of the message changes the content and meaning of the message as a whole? Convey the whole message, and nothing but the message.

I'll let you in on one of my pet peeves. If you want to blow all credibility or your chances of engaging me in a conversation again, talk *at* me as opposed to talking *with* me. After the first ten seconds of some-one talking *at* me, I simply tune out, as I imagine most others do as well. This goes back to what I said earlier about making those formal conversations as personal and relaxed as your informal ones.

When it comes to communication in the sales-person versus client arena, there is a difference between a *canned* presentation and a *planned* presentation. In a professional environment, where communication with large numbers of individuals is necessary, it is very easy to fall into a habit of certain communication habits over time. I know just about every sales organization has standard or pre-scripted dialogues their salespeople can use in their pitch. As a consumer myself, I can tell immediately when I am the two-hundredth person a phone solicitor has called that evening; it's like talking to a robot. I'm also sorry to say, I have had *face-to-face* conversations even worse than that.

We have all experienced firsthand the fake smile, pseudo concern, and condescending tone of voice of those who are using us for nothing more than a sounding board for their so-called sales pitch. Thanks, but no thanks. If I want to be talked down to and belittled, I will simply forget to take the trash out. My wife already has her script memorized for that scenario.

As a *public* speaker, it was my job to fake sincerity. As a *personal* speaker, your job is to show *real* sincerity, even if you have to write down and practice the words ahead of time.

Another important element of effective communication is *humor*. As a public speaker, I have learned over the years that people will pay far more attention when being *entertained* than they do when being *informed*. Humor is universal. It's something we all respond to. It's also a great rapport builder and icebreaker—and in some cases can even get you out of a speeding ticket.

Authors Note: I got pulled over for speeding in Los Angeles. The officer walked up to my window intending to write me a ticket. I told him I just read a magazine article listing the top ten excuses you can give a police officer to get out of a traffic ticket—but unfortunately I could only remember *one* of them right now. He stopped writing the ticket, looked at me and asked, "Oh yeah, which one's that?" And I say, "I'm in labor and I'm speeding to the emergency room!." He chuckled, told me to have a "safe delivery," closed his ticket book, walked back to his patrol car, and drove away—true story.

"Drawing upon my fine command of the English language—I said nothing."

ROBERT BENCHELY

CHAPTER 18: THE SELLING PROCESS

$

"The door to success is labeled, 'PUSH.'" Unknown

We discussed earlier the change in dynamics and the overall sales environment that has taken place in this new information age. The ease in which consumers can now make their purchases and the selection e-commerce offers is limitless. Consumers now use the same resources to compete with *each other* for goods and services, that we as sellers use to compete for consumers' business, as well as against each other, as providers of those goods and services.

The battlefield may have changed, but the players and tactics haven't. The good news about e-commerce is that it is still a *selling process*, just like the good old days. The revolution began when consumers began changing the way they located and purchased goods and services. This forced the sales industry to adopt the same "process" and follow those consumers to greener pastures.

The sales and marketing environment may have drastically changed, but the actual *process of selling* has changed little over the course of history. It's still just old fashioned supply and demand—finding a need and filling it.

We truly are living in the age of information, but from the sales industry standpoint, we are also living in the age of *service*. Consumers have always been the deciding factor in what constitutes a "market." They are the ultimate decision makers of which products and services they will purchase... or not. Now more than ever, they are also dictating the conditions and actual environment of where and how they locate and purchase goods and services. Consumers now *demand* increased selectivity, faster delivery, and lower prices or they'll simply take their business elsewhere.

Back in "the good old days," consumers may have *preferred* such conveniences, but *today* they expect and demand them from the organizations they choose to patronize. Companies that do not address those demands adequately now face a consumer who can easily and quickly shop elsewhere.

If today's consumers are so obsessed with convenience and quality service, then how do we explain the popularity of those giant warehouse operations that basically specialize in limited service and checkout lines a mile long?

How can today's sophisticated and informed consumer go from being treated like a prince at one store to being treated like cattle at another—and be equally happy in both? Different strokes for different folks? I don't think so. It is the *same* folks patronizing *both* operations, and getting what they need and want from each.

This represents a prime example of how flexible today's consumers are, and as a result, how quickly and *willingly* they adapt to varying selling environments…choice is good.

The Selling Process
THE APPROACH

This is the actual contact your product or service has with the consumer. It may be in the form of an advertisement, public display, individual contact by a salesperson, on a web site, or the actual purchase of the product. The approach is what the seller uses to make the consumer aware of the product while placing the product, as well as the consumer, in a direct position for purchase.

Your first contact with the consumer may make him "aware" of what you are selling, but unless he buys it right then and there, you'll need an effective selling process to make him remember you and what you're selling until he decides to buy at some point in the future.

As a provider, you must constantly strive to find new and better ways to present your product or service to the market. The market is very specific of what it wants, expects, and demands from those who desire it's much sought after business.

Do you as a provider really understand your customers? Are you using every means at your disposal for exposure? Is what you are using working? Always make *ongoing improvement*, not just success, a basic goal in all marketing programs.

THE RELATIONSHIP
A characteristic common to most relationships is the fact they are often easier to build than they are to *re-build*. As any product or service provider will attest to, once a customer is lost, he is usually lost for good. Actually, he is not lost—sooner or later one of your competitors will find him.

It is a lot harder to win *back* a lost client than it is to win him in the first place. That is why the true industry leaders go to great efforts to immediately identify and remedy any problem that exists in the relationship between themselves and their already won customers.

IDENTIFY
This is where it pays to be just as informed about the market as today's consumers are. Another crucial step in the selling process is to identify *what* you are selling, *who* you are selling it to, *how* you will sell it to them, and more importantly, *why* they should buy it from you...or even buy at all. Your selling process must address all four steps. These are all very fundamental questions that must be

answered before any advancement or corrections in your selling process can be made.

Since the needs and wants (demands) of consumers, as well as the individual markets themselves are constantly changing, and since we as providers must be constantly changing *with* them to survive, we must have a system to identify those changes as soon as they occur, if not anticipate them *before* they occur.

I suggest you spend some time thinking about the future. It's where you will be conducting the rest of your sales.

THE PRESENTATION
This is the method in which your product or service is displayed and made available to the customer. The awareness by the consumer that he *can* purchase the product or service is made during the approach stage. The decision if the customer *should* purchase is made during the presentation stage. The closing stage is the most crucial. It is where the consumer decides *if* he will make the purchase.

Later in the book, we will discuss in detail specific methods of presentation. Anyone who has ever been involved in retail sales knows the importance of product placement and presentation, especially when it comes to dealing with direct competitors. The goal in any competitive environment is to separate yourself from your competitors in a positive and memorable manner to your consumers. The name-brand leaders are keenly aware of positioning in the market place. Their goal is constantly to gain and maintain the coveted number one, or *most preferred* position. The same basic principles the *big boys* have been using on us all these years are the exact same things you as an individual can use on your buying public with the same effective results.

Your presentation projects a message not only about *what* is being sold, but also about *who* is doing the selling? The objective of an effective presentation is not just to sell your product to the customer—it's also to sell *you* to the customer. Once he makes *that* purchase, the sale should take care of itself.

An effective presentation sells the seller as much as the actual product or service being offered. If your current marketing plan is not selling enough products or services, then that may be because it's not effective enough at selling *you* first.

A majority of your marketing efforts are not only going to be directed at *selling* your products or services, but also at creating a better selling *environment* by first creating the proper image of your product or service in the minds of the consumer. Whenever the consumer has any contact with the product itself, the marketing of the product, or a representative of the product (you), the presented image must be consistent with the goals of the marketing strategy.

THE CLOSE

This is the *real* moment of truth. So, what usually happens when you as a salesperson find yourself at the moment? Do they sign on the line, which is dotted? Or do they smile and say, *"No thanks"*? Those numbers are called your Hit Ratio. In other words, the number of sales you make compared to the number of closing (selling) moments you have. To use a football analogy, how many times do you score from the red-zone? If you're not scoring enough touch-downs, then you need to either change your play calling (closing techniques) or increase the "number" of trips you make to the red-zone.

As any NFL fan knows, a trip to red-zone does not a touch-down make. Anything more than a *potential* customer is an actual one. A potential customer is just someone who increases your odds of making the sale, just as the red-zone increases (not guarantees) your odds of scoring, as opposed to any other place on the field. Your presentation gets you to red-zone. The "close" gets you in the end zone…or not.

So again, what happens to you when you get to the red-zone? Do you score a touch-down, settle for a field goal, or fumble the ball? Or even worse, let the other team take away the ball and score a touch-down themselves? Does the "potential" customer, instead of becoming an "actual" customer, put your brand down and walk away—perhaps with a competitor's brand? Do they decide *not* to decide and simply move on? Those questions are answered at the closing stage.

If the previous steps have been effectively implemented, a resulting sale is the logical conclusion of those steps. Hopefully, the question of *why* to buy you or your product has been answered by the closing stage. The closing stage must also answer the question *why now?* That's called *creating urgency*. I devote an entire chapter to closing techniques and creating urgency later in this book. The important thing to remember is that your entire selling process is focused on helping your customers reach certain decisions about you and what you're offering, then getting them to *act upon* what *they* have decided—with a little help from you of course.

> **"Never take a solemn oath. People think you mean it."**
>
> NORMAN DOUGLAS

CHAPTER 19: THE BUYING PROCESS

"Ours is a world where people have no idea what they want, but are willing to go through hell to get it."
DON MARQUIS

There is an entire step-by-step process the consumer goes through to purchase certain goods and services *before* he even realizes he will buy those goods or services in the first place. This is known as the *buying process*. It begins with the customer's first contact with your product or service, and continues right up to the point of purchase. With hopefully additional purchases in the future.

Did you ever stop to think why you choose to buy one product or service over another? My guess is that someone took the time to *sell* it to you before you ever bought it. When you go to your local store to buy a bottle of soda, I am willing to bet you know which particular brand of soda you are going to buy before you make that purchase or even enter the store. In fact, you were probably "sold" on that particular brand of soda before you even got thirsty. This is a consumer "buying process" that advertisers go to great expense and effort to create, develop, and maintain.

Whether we realize it or not, we as consumers are part of a constructed process that has conditioned us to respond to, and view in a particular way, the various products and services we purchase every day. This process is, however, a two-way street. The companies providing those products and services must respond to the consumer's needs and wants, just as we respond to their marketing efforts.

This process begins with the objectives of the provider, and culminates in establishing brand loyalty from the customer. Take Winston brand cigarette customers. They would rather, "fight than switch!" from their brand. What do you suppose happened? One day they just decided physical violence was better than smoking a different brand of cigarette? Of course not; they were "sold" on that particular brand using a proven process.

Before we discuss *how* people buy as part of that process, let's discuss *why* people buy the particular products and services they do.

NECESSITY
This is when the purchase of the product or service fulfills a particular *need* of the consumer. This of course is the ideal position any provider would want to be in—offering a product that the buying public requires or has grown to depend on, such as gasoline, food, clothing, and so on. Even though your particular product or service may be a necessity in a general sense, you still will have to battle it out with your competitors in your

specific arena. Just because you have what everyone *needs*, doesn't mean they'll *want* to buy it from you.

If you are fortunate enough to offer a product or service that your customers *must* purchase, then your primary focus toward those customers should be separating yourself from your competitors, exposing your product to the market, and making it as convenient as possible for your customers to locate and acquire.

COMFORT
Never in human history have convenience and ease been such powerful marketing tools. Not just convenience and ease in *using*, but also is locating and purchasing. Entire industries are dedicated to making human existence quicker, easier, and more convenient. You will never go broke overestimating the laziness of the buying public.

The ease and convenience of locating a product or service is just as important as ease in purchasing it. What good does it do if the consumer knows *who* you are and *what* you sell, but has no idea where to find you or it when they need to? It does a lot of good—to your competition! Your advertising dollars may be getting your competitors just as many sales as they are getting you, by creating a desire for a product or service the consumer is forced to purchase elsewhere because you are not as easy or convenient for those customers to find as your competitors are.

VANITY
Anyone who has ever purchased a fur coat, diamond ring, or convertible automobile is familiar with this concept. Are there any purchases you have made that may have been vanity or ego driven? Would another less expensive product or service have been more practical or convenient? If you have made such purchases, then someone sold those items to you long before you ever purchased them.

Whenever possible, the provider of a particular product or service must strive to make the image they present of themselves and their product one the customer remembers and feels good about. Think about how many products you as a consumer have purchased over a similar product simply because of the brand name or "image" that product presented to you. It might have been something as major as an automobile, or something as small as the type of sun glasses you wear, or even the type of beer you drink.

There's nothing cooler than selling a product that's cool to own. Examples would include automobiles, athletic shoes, and fashionable styles of clothing. In just about every industry you can think of, someone has gained the upper hand by being perceived as the leader of their designated pack.

SECURITY
This applies to peace of mind purchases. When it comes to selling the buying public on this con-

cept, there are several approaches that can be used, depending upon your particular product or service, as well as the type of consumer you are targeting. There are two effective approaches when it comes to marketing and selling security and peace of mind to the consumer.

The first approach addresses issues directly related to consumer personal safety and security, such as home or business security systems, self defense resources, as well as identity and property security. These products and services may be *desired* by the consumer but for *undesirable* purposes. Although the need and desire for these products and services is great among consumers, most of them would rather not even deal with such unpleasant issues like being harmed or robbed. That is why those who sell such products and services can break the cardinal rule of sales and scare the living day lights out of customers as an effective marketing tool. This works great for selling tickets to horror movies and it also works great for those TV commercials depicting theft or violence victims. Those commercials are designed to scare us so much that we immediately buy the product or service being offered to avoid ending up like those poor unfortunate victims on the TV. And of course we must act now…while supplies last.

Most people will go to great effort and expense to acquire even a small amount of security and peace of mind. Remember what we discussed earlier about the difference between *perceived* reality and *actual* reality. Fear, uncertainty, and anxiety are great motivators when it comes to getting consumers to purchase goods or services they really have no desire to own in the first place.

Whether the problem is real or perceived, the consumer may not be aware of the solution to their problem or even that it exists in the first place...until *someone* (like your friendly neighborhood salesperson) educates him. That is why home security system advertising not only "educates" the consumer about the *benefits* of purchasing a particular system, but also the *consequences* of *not* purchasing it.

A good example of this concept would be companies who sell residential smoke alarms. Their primary marketing tool has traditionally been the *first approach* where they appeal to the consumer on an obvious and basic level. They may use images designed to invoke negative or unpleasant feelings among the audience. Perhaps showing a home destroyed by fire and the distraught family standing at the curb in their pajamas watching helplessly as their belongings go up in smoke. Then a firefighter appears and says the smoke alarm saved their lives or a lack of one almost cost them theirs. Followed by, "Don't let this happen to you." At which point the consumer's fears are addressed by providing the solution—purchase one of our smoke alarms.

The smoke alarm example depicts an "obvious" problem to the consumer. But what about problems the consumer needs to be "educated" about? A great example would again be the manufacturers of smoke alarms who expanded their *existing* product line to address a *new* danger—carbon monoxide and radon. As a consumer yourself, you probably understand the importance, the need and the consequences of installing (or not) working smoke alarms in your home. But did you even know about carbon monoxide or radon before the smoke alarm companies began *educating* you about the presence and dangers of such toxins? Of course, once they did, they then "educated" you about where to buy the solution to that problem. It wasn't ease or convenience that made us all rush out and buy those detectors; it was *fear*.

The approach I just described is commonly referred to as the *fear of loss technique*. Many advertisers and providers use this with great success. Fear, as well as *fear of loss*, is one of the most effective motivational tools when it comes to influencing and directing human behavior.

A perfect example of the *second approach* is found with the same companies that have so successfully used the first approach; companies selling smoke alarms. They used the fear of loss technique to successfully sell their products, but as in many industries, certain *ceilings* exist when it comes to increasing market share. The second approach deals with creating a *new* market where one previously did not exist, as in the case of the smoke alarm companies now offering carbon monoxide and radon detectors. The exact same customers, but a whole new *market*.

They capitalized on the lack of knowledge by the consumer, educated them solely from the standpoint of a potential buyer for their product, and then offered *their* solution. Expanding your product or service offerings is a lot easier than expanding your consumer base. Your best option to gain more market share is to share more with that market.

Successful businesses always find ways of not only gaining new market share but also expanding on their existing client base as well. This can come in the form of a new niche or approach toward the consumer, or simply improving upon what you are already offering—competing against yourself so to speak. Detergent companies are famous for this. Just when they have spent countless advertising dollars convincing us their "current" product cannot be beaten, they themselves come up with a *new and improved* version of their own product that makes the previous unbeatable offering pale in comparison.

TRUST
This is the most difficult marketing station to attain. However, if you are one of those salespeople lucky (or hard working) enough having gained the like and trust of your customers, then you have successfully separated yourself from about 99 percent of your competitors.

You may have noticed that a common trend among nationally known fast food operations is to offer a new product on a regular basis for a limited time only. As consumers, new and improved appeals to our desire for variety and change. Since consumers can sometimes be skeptical when it comes to trying something new, even from a familiar and trusted source, how do these organizations successfully sell unfamiliar and perhaps un-trusted *new* products as successfully as their existing products? The product itself may be new and unfamiliar to the consumer, but they are willing to overcome such objections because they are familiar with and trust the company providing the new offering. Again, consumers must first buy *you* before they'll buy what you're selling...new and improved or not.

Even a TV commercial selling a hamburger will spend more time selling the food chain than they do the hamburger. They do that constantly to reinforce the trust and confidence the consumers associate with the company, in the hope that trust will carry over to the product or service the company is offering at the time. In other words, If you like and trust a company for what it has offered in the past, then most likely you will transfer those same attitudes toward whatever products or services they currently offer or will introduce in the future.

Remember when generic packaging was first introduced? Providers were faced with the dilemma of marketing a product that didn't even have a name…or a famous athlete or talking tiger on the box. What they did was absolute genius! Instead of asking the public to "trust" that the generic products were *better* than the competition's (like every other seller in the world has to do), they simply asked the public to trust that the generic products were only *as good as* the competition's…at half the price. Genius!

Since the buying process is based more on perception than reality, consumers are not only paying for the products and services themselves, but they are also paying for the "trust" they have in those products or services, as well as in those who provide them. Trusting customers will often buy whatever the company they trust recommends, even if it's new and unfamiliar to them. That's why the truly successful sales organizations out there spend as much time, effort, and expense building their reputation as they do their bottom line, which is of course one and the same.

The word *process* itself implies a series of events that have a pre-established start and finish. There are seven key steps to the buying process.

1. **First contact: Otherwise known as** *the moment of truth*, **you never get a second chance to make a first impression. In the business of sales, that "first impression" may have to take place** *several times* **before the impact is sufficient enough to successfully lead to the second step, which is** *recognition*. **This also means "recogni-**

tion" of not just the product or service but also of the salesperson as well. Can your customers pick you out of a lineup?

Whenever there is an introductory effort into a market, whether it be with a new product or service or entering into a new market with an existing product or service, how that introduction is received by the market will directly determine how you and it are received from basically that point forward...forever. So get it right the first time!

2. **Recognition: As stated earlier, this level will probably require several exposure opportunities to establish. If you're lucky and if what you're selling is memorable enough, this level may be achieved from the very first contact consumers have with you or your particular product or service. This is usually the exception rather than the rule. Brand recognition is most often the result of an ongoing campaign of awareness and promotion. Many products or services take years of repetitive effort to achieve recognition among their consumers. In the case of marketing an individual salesperson or provider, this level can be achieved with the first contact *if* the proper resources and strategies are utilized effectively. However, if your main goal is quantity rather than quality, you may have to sacrifice some personal or rapport building contact in exchange for higher volume prospecting. Remember, seeing is not recognizing and recognizing is not knowing. Just because the buying public knows who you are does not mean that they will ever like, trust, or even buy from you in the future.**

3. **Knowledge: This is considered what is achieved after a certain level of awareness has developed between you, your product or service, and the market place. The consumers know you, they know what you do or offer, and they know where they can find you when they need to. This is the level where your competitors will probably begin their attacks against you or the product/service you represent. In many cases, they may have no choice, especially if your efforts are proving successful and having an impact on the market.**

Once a level of consumer knowledge has been attained, you have entered the realm of being *established*. That's the first step to becoming number one. Your competitors' main focus will be making sure that you don't become *entrenched*. Once you are able to get to a level of entrenchment within your market place, your competitors will have to refocus their efforts from a defensive posture to an offensive (more expensive) one since you now hold the high ground. You must get the attention of the buying public *before* you get the attention of the competition.

4. **Likeability: We talked earlier about offering a product or service that would be purchased out of need rather than want, and the associated advantages of having a motivated buying public at your disposal. But what if your product or service is something most people could do without? What if you sell luxury items that people had to be convinced to buy, especially higher end items such as automobiles or real estate? This is where the "likeability" stage becomes crucial.**

Granted, most people *want* to own a luxury automobile...until it comes time to write the check. That's usually when they suddenly prefer that forty thousand dollars sitting in their bank account as opposed to their driveway.

There are various ways of dealing with negative perceptions by the public that may exist regarding your service, product, or industry as a whole. But on an individual level, you can still gain a certain acceptance, if not likeability when it comes to your relationship with your customers.

5. **Trust: Once you earn the customer's trust you are then in a position to earn his business. Trust is earned—and it takes time.—but it can be lost in seconds.**

Every level of your marketing and presentation must reinforce the belief that you and your product can be trusted to deliver exactly what the customer expects and the claims those expectations are based upon. As a salesperson for that product or service, you are the primary generator and source of that trust. No sale is made until trust or rapport has been established on some level.

There is no magic bullet or template for establishing trust among your customers. But it sure helps if you look, act, and talk like them. By nature, humans are suspicious of the unfamiliar or different. It tends to scare them. Even though what you're selling may be new or "unfamiliar" to the customer, you as a salesperson can "appear" familiar or at least *similar* by presenting and conducting yourself as one of them.

6. **Sold!: This part is usually the culmination of some or all of the above steps as well as other factors along the way. There are products and services offered that receive immediate success simply by being offered in the first place. Others are dependent upon advertising, market conditions, or just being in the right place at the right time. Either way, the final step for each is SOLD! Or is it?**

Some salespeople make the costly mistake of thinking that "SOLD!" is the finish line. If you really want to see your income and sales explode, not only become an expert at selling, but also at *reselling*.

7. **Repeat and referral sales: Congratulations! You have reached the pinnacle of success in the sales industry. Ideally, at this point, you have made sufficient contacts and past sales to establish an existing client base who knows who you are, what you have to offer, and where you or your product/service can be found when needed, all with a carefully crafted image of likeability and trust. Now what?**

The mark of a good salesperson is getting the sale. The mark of a *great* salesperson is getting the resale—meaning repeat or referral business. Whether it's in the form of repeat business from existing clients or referral business from existing clients, the ultimate goal is still the same. Get your customers as quickly as possible to a level of need or satisfaction that brings their business back as well as the business of those they recommend and refer to you.

The best way to get your customers back is to treat them as if you *want* them back! If you want and expect them to recommend and refer business to you, then you must take the extra step of informing them of what you want and expect in the way of future business. Trust me, they'll be more than willing and happy to do it—if they like and trust you.

This can be accomplished several ways. The first is to offer such a superior product or service that your customers naturally return to do business as well as refer business to you. The second way is by a concentrated prospecting effort toward existing markets or clients asking for and prompting them to re-buy or refer you additional business. The third way is to prompt the customer to take that extra step himself and actually go from being a customer, to a source of repeat and referral business, to a position where he actively helps direct sales to you. I've had numerous clients over the years that did that very thing. You know why? Because I got them to like and trust me—then I asked them for those referrals and repeat business. One woman actually photocopied her personal phone book and gave me all the contact info of everyone she knew and permission to contact them with her recommendation!

Most satisfied consumers will have no problem recommending a "good thing" to their friends and contacts.

> *"I believe you can get everything in life you want if you just help enough other people get what they want."*

ZIG ZIGLAR

CHAPTER 20: QUALIFYING THE PROSPECT

"Trust in yourself. Your perceptions are often far more accurate than you are willing to believe."

CLAUDIA BLACK

Proper qualifying has just as much to do with listening to the answers as it does with asking the right questions. Communication is basically the exchange of information. It entails the sending as well as the receiving of information. Which means "listening" to what the prospect is telling you as opposed to just *hearing* him.

The mark of a true salesperson is getting the prospect to make some form of commitment during the qualifying stage before they ever get to the closing stage. Many salespeople find the actual closing stage the most difficult. That burden can be eased by obtaining smaller commitments from the prospect along the way, prior to the actual asking for his business.

If you use the probing stage to educate and inform the prospect, as well as gain the necessary information to qualify him as a legitimate prospect, you will find that the closing stage becomes a lot easier.

This concept of *information exchange* versus *fact gathering* is called *Relationship Selling,* as opposed to the hard or on-the-spot sale. I've always found the average client will respond in a more positive fashion to my request for the sale when I engage him in a little non-selling dialogue first. This casual banter will insure that even if the prospect does not make the purchase right then and there, at the very least, he learns a little about you, your product, or service, and you gain the opportunity to contact him again for future or referral business. Some of the best referrals I ever received came from people to whom I never made a sale.

In order for you to maximize the results of the dialogue exchange, you must be able to direct the conversation and lead the prospect in a manner in which he does not realize he is being led or even that he's *following*. Remember, the person asking the questions is the person in control of the conversation. That of course should be *you* since you are the one who needs the information the prospect already possesses.

There is no "sale" without some form of rapport when a salesperson is involved in the selling process. There might be a *purchase*, but the goal here is *salesmanship*. "Purchases" can only make you so much money...but "salesmanship" can make you rich.

When you attempt to *romance* a potential customer, your goal is to establish a certain level of likeability, trust, or even just product knowledge. This technique is to establish a semi-personal relationship between yourself and the prospect that goes beyond the mere objective of getting him to like and purchase the product or service you are offering. The ultimate goal is to establish an atmosphere of informality and friendship.

There are as many ways to accomplish this as there are clients and salespeople combined, and each scenario must be handled on a case-by-case basis since no two prospects or salespeople are exactly the same.

Your goal is to develop your own particular style, then make the necessary adjustments along the way with each client as your level of skill, competence, and confidence grows. Naturally, you will have to stay within the guidelines of your individual market, product, or service—and of course your comfort zone.

I really want to stress the point of developing your own personal style that is both effective and *comfortable* for you. The reason I want you to develop a style that you feel comfortable with is that in most cases, the prospect can pick up on those little signals a person sends when he does not feel confident or comfortable doing what he's doing. It may only be a matter of natural closing reluctance on your part. But to a prospect, it may come across as lack of confidence in what you are trying to tell or sell them. When the prospect thinks you are trying to get him to do something you yourself may not be comfortable doing, you may lose all credibility with that client, and usually the sale as well.

Your individual style of *romancing* your prospects will come more naturally than you think. Once you begin practicing your selling and closing techniques on your clients, the more comfortable and at ease you will become at using them. After a while, they will be flowing out of you as naturally as a conversation with your closest friend. If you think about it, the most effect salespeople you as a customer may have encountered over the years were probably ones who made you feel as if they had known you for years.

Using this formula as a guideline, you should be able to accomplish your goal of properly qualifying your prospect with a natural, brief conversation. Much like a car salesperson, with just a few words—"So what can I show you today?"—the salesperson has put the customer in an immediate position to identify him, at least partially, as qualified or not. Potential customers typically give two standard answers when asked that textbook question by the car salesperson—"I'm just looking," which means they *may* be qualified and the salesperson will need to ask a few more qualifying questions; or the customer will directly answer the salesperson's question and describe what he is looking for. Without knowing anything about that customer, the salesperson quickly qualified him with one question.

Even though you may be able to quickly qualify the prospect with one or two standard introductory questions, knowing he *can* buy is not the same and knowing he *will* buy...or at least today. Here's an easy seven-step process you can use to accurately and quickly qualify most prospects.

STEP 1: Repeat and clarify; remember, the person in charge of the conversation is the one asking the questions. Naturally, the prospect may have questions too, but when directing your questions, don't just *listen* to the prospect's answers—take an active role in the conversation by *responding* to those answers as well. Whenever the prospect responds to one of your key questions, for his benefit, as well as yours, be sure you not only heard the answer but *listened* to it as well. The best way to accomplish this is by *repeating* the answer back to the prospect. This can be verbatim or close variance. Just be sure that you use as many of the prospect's *own words* as possible. This will eliminate confusion and misunderstanding.

STEP 2: Paraphrase; after you have repeated the answer back to the prospect in *his* own words, the next step is to repeat it back to him in *your* own words. Paraphrase the answer back to him, prefaced with something like, "If I'm understanding you correctly," or, "So what you are saying is...." This will confirm his initial response. Plus, it also shows you *really were* listening to what he was saying.

STEP 3: Agree; we all know the old adage, "The customer is always right"? Well, the truth is, most times they are *not* right. In fact, they are often anything but right. That is where you and your selling skills come into play. This in no way implies that you tell the customer he is wrong. It means using your skill and salesmanship to get him to see things from another point of view—one necessary to make the sale. Be sure to use terms such as, "I agree," and "That's correct," to let him know you understand and agree with his point of view…*for now.*

STEP 4: Exchange information; this step has two objectives. The first is to put you in charge of the conversation by being the one asking the leading questions; and second, this is where you obtain the necessary information regarding the prospect's particular need and motivation to make the purchase or not (qualified). If the prospect is not qualified to make the purchase, or not to make the purchase *right now*, you need to identify that fact as quickly as possible.

I have found the most effective way to get the client to respond positively to my questions and provide me the necessary information about himself, is to make my conversation with him seem as non-business as possible. I would often ask questions that had nothing to do with the sale, as well as tell him little personal tidbits about myself. I find that most prospects appreciate being dealt with on a personal basis at least initially. Even in a business situation. Be sure to show genuine concern not only for the clients' needs and wants but for them as individuals as well. When they notice this level of communication, they will be more open and honest with you as well as more likely to buy.

STEP 5: *Listen*; I have seen some of the most successful salespeople in the business talk themselves *into* a sale and then talk themselves right out of it. Once you ask a leading or closing question, your job at that point is to shut up and listen.

Sometimes your ability to make the sale or not will be entirely dependent upon the mood of the customer at the time. A person's physical gestures can tell you more about his mood than his actual words. Most of us are better at guarding our words than we are our actions. It is very important to listen with more than just your ears. Take notice of not only *what* the prospect is saying but *how* he is saying it. His physical gestures, tone of voice, and certain words or phrases can give you important insights into the prospect's mood or how your message is being received (see chapter 17 on Effective Communication.)

STEP 6: Anticipate; any salesperson that has direct contact with prospects more than likely encounters his fair share of standard objections and *brush-offs* he hears on a regular basis. After you have been in the business for a while, you will begin to see certain patterns regarding sales made and sales lost. After a while, you will be able to "anticipate" what the majority of those objections will be before the clients actually voice them. You cannot predict *every* reason a prospect can give as to why he won't or can't buy what you are trying to sell him, but I would bet there are several you probably hear on a regular basis. Anticipate and plan for those common objections.

The first place to begin when it comes to anticipating, then hopefully overcoming, the objections you may encounter is to put yourself in your clients' shoes. Try to see things strictly from their standpoint. Remember, those prospects probably do not have the same level of knowledge or confidence in your product or service as you do, in fact, they may even arrive with pre-established negative preconceptions regarding you, your industry, or particular product or service. Ask your organization's management, trainer, or some of the more experienced salespeople in your organization and I bet they can provide you a list of the top five or ten objections they usually encounter. Hopefully, they're also willing to share with you their most effective techniques for overcoming those objections.

I would suggest you compile a list of the most common objections you or your particular sector encounter on a regular basis. In fact, make a list of *every* objection you have ever encountered. Trust me...sooner or later you'll hear them all again. The next step is to write out a sample dialogue that you can recite in a confident comfortable manner to handle each objection. That will be your objection-handling arsenal. The best method for anticipating objections, then effectively overcoming them, is also the same way you get to Carnegie Hall—practice; don't worry. You won't be the first salesperson to lock the bathroom door and stand in front of the mirror talking to imaginary clients—that look exactly like you.

STEP 7: Mirror the prospect; ideally, you should begin to mirror the prospect's body language, gestures, and voice tone from the very beginning of your presentation and continue throughout until the final closing stage.

One of the oldest sales techniques in the book is the "Chameleon Technique," which is exactly what it implies—duplicating the mannerisms, gestures and body language of the prospect in order to create the perception in his mind of, "Hey. This person is just like me. I guess I can trust him."

The qualifying stage is primarily to give you enough information about the prospect's motivations and desires to put you in control during the conversation and increase your chances of closing the sale. The qualifying stage of course should ultimately lead to the closing stage. It is an opportunity to get the *little closes* so to speak out of the way before moving on to the big close—asking for the sale.

What exactly do I mean by "the little closes?" If you can get the prospect to answer "yes" regarding small items in your presentation then you have him pre-conditioned, so to speak, to give you that big "yes" when you ask for the sale—much like getting him to put his feet in the water before diving in head first. Those little yeses are referred to as "soft closes" (as opposed to the "hard sell"). With every little "yes" the prospect gives to your probing questions, he moves one step closer to that final big yes.

The most effective probing sessions are those that are conducted in an informal and friendly manner, even if it means sticking to the script.

Here are some tips you can use to make your probing sessions at least *seem* more personal and friendly.

1. **Get permission to ask: I strongly recommend, even as a matter of formality, you get the prospect's permission before asking him any significant questions. Besides, it's common courtesy. It's not only a common courtesy but also a perfect chance to get one of those little yeses out of the way.**

2. **Ask the questions: If you have a written list of prepared questions, then simply read them off the list. Expanding and paraphrasing where necessary. As long as the prospect understands that you are following a pre-established process and not just making this up as you go along, it will seem like the normal and established**

buying process for your particular product or service. Prospects understand that a salesperson asking a buyer questions to find out exactly what he's looking for comes with the territory.

3. **Recap the answers:** This is the technique we discussed earlier when it comes to paraphrasing and repeating responses back to the client for clarification. Even if you understand, or *think* you understand the prospect's answer, repeat it back to him. Then finish by saying something like, "Is that correct?" This will once again give you another little "yes" along the way.

4. **Write down the answers (if possible or practical):** First of all, writing down shows that you are listening and that you care about what they are telling you. Second, the prospect will appreciate it. There is nothing worse than speaking to someone who looks as if he's *somewhere else* or not actively paying attention. You can also use such techniques as writing down the answers to help keep you focused and on track during your presentation. If you are anything like I was as a salesman, sometimes I would get so caught up in trying to make the sale I wasn't really listening to the answers my prospects were giving as much as focusing on what I was going to say when they finished their sentence.

Here's another reason to write things down; our memories are terrible! Face it, how can you remember something you weren't listening to in the first place? If you stick to a list of pre-planned questions and record the prospect's answers *as they are given*, it will eliminate the need to focus more intensely on certain aspects of the dialogue in the hope of better remembering them later. Writing down the answers frees up your mind, so to speak, and allows you to keep flowing mentally with the conversation.

The more effective your qualifying process is, the faster you can separate *real* clients from merely potential ones or *just-lookers*. The faster and easier you can accomplish that task, the more potential clients you have to time to sift through trying to identify the "real" ones among the potential ones. Some salespeople are so adept at their individual qualifying process that they can spot a qualified customer without ever having to engage him in conversation.

A good salesperson gets the sale while at the same time getting better at getting the next one.

"There is no right way to do something wrong."

UNKNOWN

CHAPTER 21: THE PRESENTATION

If your intention is to convince a customer to part with his hard earned money, it may take a little more than reading cue cards. Therein lies the difference between a *canned* presentation and a *planned* presentation. When it comes to what some refer to as their *sales pitch*, it's all in the delivery. This is where your selling skills and instincts really come into play. The true salesperson can tailor those skills almost instantly to better adapt to his individual clients or selling situations.

Most sales professionals posses some degree of natural as well as learned salesmanship skills when it comes to interacting with prospects. For most sales professionals, their selling techniques were probably first developed in some kind of training or practice environment before being applied in the field on actual clients. As most instructors will admit, you cannot learn skill in a classroom or from a book. What you *can* learn, however, is the processes and strategies for applying what you learn in the classroom to the actual selling situations you encounter in the field, face to face with live prospects.

As I have reinforced all along, selling is a process and every phase of that process is itself a process. My point is that if you take an individual component of the entire selling process, such as the presentation, that presentation is itself made up of a process. You can then take the individual components of the presentation process and create a formula that produces for you the desired results. That formula will of course take into account several factors such as your client base, the method of prospecting, your skills as a salesperson as well as the *variables* or individual factors concerning each scenario.

There are as many sales presentations for various products and services as there are products and services for sale. There are, however, some basic guidelines and steps that can be *generally* applied to most selling and presenting situations. Some presentations are indeed no more than reading a scripted dialogue and taking the order. Other types may require client research or a more customized approach.

If you can take into account all the variables and individualities of your particular sales environment and incorporate them into the following presentation formula, you should have an effective process you can follow not only to help you better communicate with your prospects on *their* level, but also to ensure you cover all the material necessary to give a complete presentation.

A *planned* presentation is exactly that, your *plan*. An effective *plan* ensures you will *present* all the major information necessary to inform the prospect enough about you and your product or service to create the necessary desire and motivation for him to make the purchase. The plan will work—if you will work the plan. If you're out there *winging it* or giving a presentation with no pre-structured plan or specific objectives other than getting the sale, then it's like giving your sales pitch for the very first time over and over again.

That is why you must pre-establish a repeated *process* using what you know works with your particular clients and market. The real key is to make your repetitive process come across as spontaneous and natural with each individual client. Just because you happen to be saying something for the one hundredth time that day doesn't mean it has to *sound* like it.

The Sales Presentation Process

1. **Break the ice: This can be as simple as an introduction or handshake. Personally, I always try to use a compliment of some kind. Trust me, you can always find a reason to compliment someone,** *if you look hard enough.* **For example, when prospecting as a door-to-door salesperson, I came to this one house that had a sign on the front door saying, "Watch where you step! 15 cats live here." After I rang the doorbell, I had about thirty seconds to**

think of a compliment for someone, who for whatever reason, owned fifteen cats! And believe it or not, I actually thought of one just as she was answering the door! "Hello ma'am. I see you own fifteen cats. Gee...it smells like only ten from out here." Like I said, you can *always* find a reason to compliment someone. A sincere compliment delivered in a sincere manner is the *perfect* ice breaker. Start approaching potential customers like that every time and watch your sales skyrocket!

(Author's Note: I am about to teach you something that can double your sales literally overnight; it did mine. Did you laugh at the above cat lady example? If so, then you are eight times more likely to remember it. From now on, every time you encounter a potential customer, before you say a word to them, I want you to say to yourself, "fifteen cats." Those trigger-words will remind you to identify an "ice breaker" compliment before you approach the prospect.)

2. **Establish Rapport: The first step in the rapport establishing and building process is to find a common bond between yourself and the prospect. If you are unable to quickly identify something you have in common with the prospect, such as them wearing a ball cap with your favorite team's logo on it, then do like I said above, quickly identify a way to** *compliment* **them.**

This common bond can be the reason you are approaching them in the first place, or even related to the product or service you are offering. In a more prolonged environment, something in your ice breaking conversation with the prospect may indicate a common interest or situation. For instance, many times I would visit clients to make a sales proposal and notice they had a fish aquarium displayed in their home or office. In particular, I would look for saltwater displays. I too have a saltwater aquarium in my office. I got it based on the recommendations of my doctor who said it was a great tool for relieving stress. It has become the most expensive and time consuming nightmare I have ever encountered, to say the least, *causing me a great deal of stress!* You'd be surprised at what a common bond my dealings with that ridiculous tank are to other saltwater aquarium owners. Plus, that scenario is based on one of the greatest selling techniques of all time—*humor.*

3. **Ask permission to begin: You will often hear salespeople say, "May I show you how it works?" or "Can I tell you more about it?" many times** *after* **they've already begun showing or telling you. Once you have the prospect's permission to begin your sales presentation, do not stop until you have said everything you plan to say, or the client says "sold!"**

4. **Take control: Leadership is easy, if you're willing to assume it—but once you lose it, it's very difficult to regain. Once you relinquish control of the conversation then you must wrestle it back from the client, which automatically puts you in an adversarial position. You may even come across as rude.**

Keep the dialogue flowing along a pre-planned course by setting up each follow-up question with the preceding one. Following this formula should keep you on track and in control throughout the entire presentation.

Probe the Prospect: The information and facts you gather about the prospect and his situation during this phase of the process will dictate not only the balance of your presentation, as well as the type of close you'll be using, but quite possibly whether or not you even make the sale. How can you find out what the client likes, wants or needs without asking him in some form or another? Or you can give your entire presentation only to find out after you have finished that the prospect is not ready, willing, or even able to make the purchase. The probing session can also be the *elimination* session.

6. **Find a problem: The first potential problem is that the prospect doesn't yet own what you're selling. And if what you're selling happens to be something the prospect needs or wants, but does not yet have...***that's a problem.* **Show me a person with a problem and I'll show you a customer. That's your main focus as a salesperson, to find that need or want or problem. Once you've identified the "problem," it's time to move on to the next step.**

7. **Offer the solution: That solution, hopefully, is you or your product's or service's ability to solve the previously identified problem.**

Any salesperson worth his or her salt should, at the very least, be able to tell a prospect why he should buy his particular product or service. If you cannot think of a good reason, don't expect the prospect to.

8. **Close for the sale: You knew we'd get to this step sooner or later. There are as many ways to close a client for the sale as there are clients to close. This is where your skill, instincts, and product/service knowledge all come into play. A natural sense of timing doesn't hurt either. Now let us say the prospect is unfamiliar with his part in this little scene and somehow blows his lines. For instance, he does something stupid like say he is willing to buy after you've only completed steps one and two of your presentation. Then what? Listen carefully;** *forget about steps three through eight***! Your presentation is over! Done! Finished! The only thing left is step nine: collect the money.**

You have no idea how many salespeople, out of some warped sense of commitment I guess, pass up the opportunity to close the sale right then and there rather than risk the client missing even one reason why he should buy. Like I said, I've seen salespeople talk themselves into a sale only to talk themselves right out of it! Let me say it again. Once the client agrees to buy what you're selling, *your presentation is over*. The entire purpose of the presentation is to talk the client into buying. If he's already at that point, shut up and show him where to sign.

I have tried to be as specific as possible when dealing with the generalities of a sales presentation regarding a salesperson, client, product, or

service. I know *selling*—and I know what works...
most of the time. So you will need to fill in the rest
of the blanks regarding your particular situation
based on your own experiences. There are, however, some other general rules that apply to most
buyer-seller relationships.

Rule #1: The sheep know what the wolf wants, no
matter how much you sugar coat it. You know it;
they know it. Sooner or later it all boils down to,
"Do you want to buy?" I find most clients appreciate you getting to the point as quickly as possible.
Your time may be their money. Nothing is worse
or more annoying than a salesperson who spends
the entire presentation beating around the bush. I
think I speak for customers everywhere when I say,
"Get to the point!"

Rule #2: Stay focused on the objective—the sale.
In other words, don't lose sight of the forest for the
trees. Your purpose is to convince the prospect to
buy what you're selling in the most pleasant and
timely manner possible. All dialogue should cen-
ter around that main concept. Everything you say
and do should progress the client toward the sale.
How can you expect the client to stay focused on
the objective if you can't? Believe me; many times
the prospect is looking for a way out of the selling
situation. Don't open the door for him by getting
off the subject of buying.

Rule #3: Avoid *shop talk*. There is nothing more
uncomfortable or a bigger turnoff for a prospect

than being talked to with words, terms, and phrases he doesn't know the meaning of. Once you say something the prospect doesn't understand, you have lost him, you have lost control of the conversation and possibly your credibility as well as the sale. If you tailor your presentation to the level of the *least* informed consumer you will be dealing with, then you should effectively reach the rest of your client base. Most successful salespeople have several levels of communication depending on the individual situation or client.

Rule #4: Emphasize value over price. They are not one in the same. The price is what the consumer will pay. The value is what the product or service is *worth* to that client, regardless of cost. A great example would be those who sell Rolls Royce automobiles. The primary focus of their presentation I would imagine, would probably be to direct the buyer *away* from the price and more toward the *value* of owning the finest automobile in the world as opposed to *paying* for one.

Rule #5: Don't compete with distractions. Even though as a salesperson you may be working at the time, if your sales presentation is taking place in your prospect's work environment, try to have his calls and interruptions held until your presentation is over. This is not too much to ask. If you are dealing with consumers in a more personal or home environment it is always advisable to be as far away from the children and/or television set as possible.

If you find yourself dealing with clients in mostly a personal environment, you can do some things to create a more business-like atmosphere. Although you are in someone's home and not his office, chances are they do conduct business there to some extent, even if it is just sitting at the kitchen table paying bills once a month. I think you will also find that even if it is just once a month, when those prospects are at that kitchen table they are more in a business frame of mind than while sitting on the couch trying to listen to you and Homer Simpson at the same time.

The business of selling is almost hectic by nature. Sometimes the best you can hope for is a lull in the action or some kind of control over the chaos.

Rule #6: Every presentation is canned. The good ones just don't sound like it. How do you get your *planned* presentation to sound natural and less "canned"? Practice!

Rule #7: Approach every prospect with the attitude of, "Give it your best shot," as opposed to, "Don't shoot!" Unless you are selling bottled water in the middle of the desert, there will probably be some form of objection handling required during your presentation. Expect it, and more importantly *plan for it.*

Rule #8: Push *why* over *what.* Give the client enough reasons *why* to buy, and *what* you are selling will take care of itself. The client doesn't particularly care exactly what the product or service is as long as he has a good enough reason to buy it. How many items are in your home right now that you bought because it sounded like a good idea at the time?

Before a consumer pays for anything, he usually asks himself at some point, *What's in it for me?* The key is to answer that question as part of your presentation before the prospect even thinks to ask.

Rule #9: Different strokes are for different folks. Although the particular product or service you are selling may remain the same, each individual client and selling situation will be different to some extent. At the very least, you will be dealing with different types of clients; while some may react more to visual approaches, others will respond more positively to audio or kinesthetic methods. Then of course, there are the different personality types and selling environments, not to mention every individual need, want, or problem needing to be addressed.

Rule #10: Say everything you need to say with as few words as possible. Sometimes half a presentation is better than no presentation, but sometimes it can be worse. If there is not sufficient time to do everything you have to do and say everything you have to say in order for that consumer to make an informed decision whether or not to buy your product, then if at all possible reschedule the appointment to a better time…or talk real fast.

I recommend having an abbreviated version of your presentation always at the ready for just such instances. Just be sure you do not abbreviate it too much. Remember, the client probably doesn't know as much regarding your product or service as you do. By leaving some things out, you may only convey enough information to the prospect to talk him *out* of the sale.

"I hate quotes. Tell me what you know."

RALPH WALDO EMMERSON

CHAPTER 22: OVERCOMING OBJECTIONS

"I know God will not give me anything I can't handle. I just wish he didn't trust me so much."

MOTHER TERESA

Take it from a former used car salesman, people don't kick the tires or point out the dents on a car they aren't at the very least *thinking* about buying. When a potential customer would start pointing out the flaws of a particular vehicle, or better yet complaining about the price, I knew he would be driving it home within the hour! Who cares about a small scratch on a car or what it costs if you are not at least considering purchasing it? If you haven't already figured this out, let me share a little secret with you: *objections are your friends*—treat them accordingly. They give you tremendous insight into what the customer is thinking; not to mention the fact that objections are the greatest *buying* signals a prospect can give you, *if* you know how to recognize those signals.

We discussed in the previous chapter the importance of developing an attitude toward your prospects of, "Give it your best shot!" as opposed to, "Don't shoot!" or an attitude of, "Go ahead and ask," instead of, "I hope they don't ask me about that." You cannot go into a selling situation *gun shy.* When it comes to selling or interacting with clients, 99 percent of your anticipated fears will prove unfounded. In no other industry is the phrase "We have nothing to fear but fear itself" more applicable.

Just as your sales training and experience are processes that need to be developed over time, so too are objection-handling techniques. They will evolve and become more effective over time just as you will as a salesperson.

Objection-Handling Process

Step 1: *Hear them out*; this is something it took me years as a salesperson to learn. Half of all the objections you here from a customer will be little more than idle chatter. Most of the rest are buying signals. That means half of all the objections you hear from prospects will require no more than step 1 (hearing them out).

Step 2: *Acknowledge and Repeat*; this will confirm to the prospect as well as to yourself that you fully understand the customer's concern. It may seem like a minor objection to *you* but a major one to the prospect, or vice-versa. Possible verbiage might be, "I understand your reluctance because of..." (repeat objection back to prospect).

Step 3: *Show concern, sincere* concern; nothing will isolate or turn off a prospect faster than the realization his concerns are secondary to you. If his objection is important to him, then it should be equally important to you. Possible verbiage here might be, "If I were in your shoes that would be important to me too."

Step 4: *Cushion it*; while at the same time conveying importance and concern for the objection, you must also try to minimize or downplay the objection in a manner that doesn't appear as dismissive to the prospect. This can be a little tricky. You do not want to just dismiss an issue the client sees as important, but on the other hand, you don't want the mole hill to become a mountain either. Your facial expressions during this step are very important, even more so than your actual words. Now may be a good time to practice that *concerned* look in the mirror.

When a prospect does indicate a concern, it will be up to you to accurately assess how valid that concern is. Of course, in his mind, every concern he has is valid. But some concerns are more valid than others. As I said before, sometimes they're just engaging in conversational back and forth or letting you know they are paying attention or have some knowledge about your product or service. Sometimes a cigar is just a cigar.

If they repeat a certain concern, or fail to move beyond it, then you may be dealing with a concern that is more valid than the others, and one that needs to be addressed in some way. It is important at this stage for you to try and gauge the prospect's *real* level of concern as best you can. If he seems sincerely concerned about something, then it may take a little more *cushion* than other objections. Just be sure not to lean too far in the other direction by turning the speed bump into a road block. Possible verbiage might be, "I think you'll see, once I explain..." (then use the appropriate verbiage to downplay the concern). Most of the time, it's going to be a simple matter of clarification on a particular point.

Step 5: *Isolate it*; you must separate or isolate the objection from the selling process before you can successfully overcome it. You must make the concern or objection a separate issue from the presentation *or the sale*. That will give you the golden opportunity not only to handle the concern but also to turn it into an opportunity to close for the sale.

Isolating the objection as a separate issue from the sale is simple. Here it goes, "Is there anything else keeping you from buying?" If their answer is *yes* then repeat this same process with each additional objection or concern as they occur.

If the prospect answers, *"no,"* then stay on track, overcome the objection, and make the sale.

Step 6: *Write it down*; this step is used more in formal, negotiation style selling situations. If there is a fairly large dollar amount involved with the purchase, then by all means address every aspect in detail. By writing the objection down, you will convey to the prospect your genuine concern for his position as well show him you see the situation from his perspective. This is crucial during any negotiating stage.

Step 7: *Question it*; you must ask yourself if what the client has said is indeed an objection that must be handled or a concern that can be minimized. Is the customer simply stalling before making a commitment (usually the case) or is it a true condition (roadblock) of the sale? If you've been selling your particular product or service for any length of time, you probably are a little familiar with some standard objections you hear on a recurring basis. You also probably know which ones deserve greater attention than others. If the concern or objection is *real*, then you must overcome it to the customer's satisfaction before making the sale or continuing with your presentation.

Step 8: *Address it*; if by this point, you have a legitimate objection or condition on your hands, then this is where the rubber meets the road. This is the part of selling that requires *salesmanship*. And salesmanship is what separates salespeople from order takers. It's also what puts them in a higher tax bracket.

Here's a simple phrase you can use to qualify your buyer quickly, handle most objections, and get the customer to put his money where his mouth is: "If I could… would you?" In other words, if you can successfully overcome his objection, will he buy? Yes or no? Put up or shut up --- which is exactly what you do after you ask one of the greatest closing questions of all time.

If on the other hand the concern the prospect has raised cannot be successfully overcome then you have what's called a *condition* of the sale. Then it is no longer a case of whether or not he *wants* to buy as much as it is *can* or should he buy. This is where your professional *higher calling* comes in. If you believe the customer will not benefit from the purchase, or worse yet be hurt by it, then do not make the sale. Remember the part about always putting the customer first.

Step 9: *Confirm the answer*; remember, you just asked them a *closing question*. Actually you just asked them "*the*" closing question—"Will you buy?" And once you ask a closing question, you know what to do; shut up and wait for an answer. If you've done your job and the prospect is qualified, you should be hearing a "yes." But what happens if the answer they give is not *yes*?

Sometimes you're going to hear the word "no." And anything but a *yes* is a *no*. If you do get a no, or other variation, nod your head like you understand, then follow up with the standard, "May I ask why?" I'm serious! Don't be shy about asking them why not? I hate to point out the obvious but what have you got to lose? At this point, you technically have *no sale*. Just get it over with and ask them *why not*—then as usual, shut up and listen to their answer. I'll let you in on a little secret why it's so important to ask that follow-up question of *why not*. Most of the time their answer will be something like, "Oh I don't know…" And then they'll say, "OK…I'll buy." You'll see.

So what if the answer is a "yes"? Congratulations, you just made a sale!

I have given you a sales industry standard formula for addressing, handling, and overcoming objections and hesitancy on the part of your prospects. Naturally each prospect, salesperson, and selling situation is different, and as a result, your various approaches to those clients and situations will also be different—but yet the same. *Handle* each client differently, but *treat* each of the same.

There are basically four ways you can handle most objections:

Number 1: Before they occur. This is called *proactive*. As I said earlier, there are probably several objections and concerns you encounter on a fairly regular basis. If there is a legitimate concern you anticipate being brought up, I recommend getting that skeleton out of the closet right up front. If you are dealing with a legitimate condition of the sale then it's better to identify it *before* your presentation.

Number 2: As they occur. This is called *reactive*. This is basically your job description in a nutshell—dealing with problems *as they occur*. Just remember to stick to the objection-handling process we discussed earlier.

Number 3: Later. This approach is mainly used on minor objections and stalls. A simple "I understand" or "I'll get to that in a minute" should suffice. Then continue your presentation. But if it *is* a major concern or a condition then use the objection-handling process to address it immediately.

Number 4: Never. This one's my favorite. Unfortunately, it only works on *minor* objections and stalls. As I mentioned earlier, some objections you get will require nothing more than a nod of the head and a sincere, "I understand." Show concern... then move on. Which is basically the "Never" approach.

There are as many objection-handling techniques as there are salespeople. My guess is that your particular industry has figured out most of them long before you showed up. In fact, they're probably laying around your sales office somewhere. I'm serious! Next time you're in the office, check out the training materials for the new salespeople. Try looking under the category "Common objections you'll face selling _____ and how to effectively handle them." If you work in an office full of *low producers*, bring a dust rag; you may have to wipe some cobwebs off those materials.

Not every objection-handling technique is going to work every time, but *some* will work *some* of the time. However, if you fail to master and implement them, they will of course work *none* of the time.

To successfully handle most concerns by the prospect, you must get to the real reason for the objection. That's your job when confronted with any hesitation by the customer, to identify the *real* problem, despite what the customer says. Are you dealing with a stall, an objection, or an actual condition? Keep probing until you can answer that question to your own satisfaction.

The Stall: This is a common occurrence in some form or another among many buyers. It's just a normal reaction to reaching into their wallet or checkbook. In fact, I always thought there must be a school somewhere teaching it. The stall is the reason they *give* you why they can't buy. Your job at this point is to say to yourself, "They're lying," and move on to the next step, which is to probe the prospect until you get to the *real* objection.

The Real Objection: This is the reason they *believe* why they can't buy. Your job at this point is to probe further to determine if you are indeed dealing with an objection or an actual condition of the sale.

The Condition: This is the *real* reason they can't or won't buy. If there is a real reason why they can't or shouldn't buy, you should discover this during the initial probing session and not during or, worse, at the *end* of your presentation. If through your probing you determine you are dealing with only an objection, then use the objection-handling process to overcome it. If on the other hand you determine that you are dealing with a bona fide condition preventing the prospect from making the purchase, thank him for his time and move on to the next prospect. The faster you get through this process, the more time you will have to convert qualified prospects into qualified customers.

There are usually four general categories most objections will fall into.

1. **The money**

2. **The product or service**

3. **You**

4. **They're still not convinced.**

If you're looking for a real gutsy close, then go ahead and ask them which one of the four it is. About 90 percent of the time, they will go ahead and tell you. At which point, you direct the objection-handling process to the one (hopefully only one) they picked of the four until they *are* convinced.

To some salespeople, this is going to seem like the hardest part of selling. Take it from me; it doesn't have to be. There is a silver lining to this cloud, actually a *golden* one. Successful sales contain 50 percent more objections than unsuccessful ones do. Like I said earlier, people don't kick the tires of a car they are not thinking of buying. So from now on when you hear an objection or stall from a prospect, you should be thinking…SOLD!

In fact, statistically speaking, and as we will discuss later in the chapter on Closing Techniques, you will often have to hear the word "no" seven times before you hear the word "*yes*." So the next time you hear a "no," just think…one down, six more to go!

"It's not the situation. It's your reaction to the situation."

BOB CONKLIN

CHAPTER 23: NEGOTIATING

Jane Hathaway: "Chief, haven't you ever heard of the old saying it's not whether you win or lose, it's how you play the game"?

Mr. Drysdale: "Yes, I've heard of it. And I consider it one of the most ridiculous statements ever made."
                              THE BEVERLY HILLBILLIES (TV SERIES)

A man visits an insane asylum and is given a tour by one of the doctors. The first patient they encounter is just sitting there staring out the window crying. The visitor asks the doctor what's wrong with the patient. The doctor explains that his fiancée left him at the altar and ran off with another man. The next patient they encounter is locked in a padded cell, wearing a straight jacket and screaming wildly at the top of his lungs. The visitor asks the doctor what his problem is. The doctor replies, "That's the guy the other patient's fiancée ran off with."

Negotiating rule number one: Sometimes the best deal is the one you *don't* make.

Many of the negotiating techniques and strategies I'll be sharing with you are based on concepts you learned in the chapter on Effective Communication. As far as I'm concerned, negotiating and communication are pretty much one in the same.

If you can effectively communicate with others then you can learn the art of effective negotiating as well.

Negotiating is basically an exchange of dialogue and ideas between two or more individuals, directed toward a common goal of achieving a mutually acceptable agreement between the parties.

Based on the above definition, we are "negotiating" all the time, in professional as well as personal situations. Once you learn how to control and direct those interactions with others, you will be able to lead them more often than not, into accepting what you desire as the end result.

I recommend first applying the techniques you are about to learn on your personal or non-selling contacts; it's cheaper than practicing and developing your negotiating techniques with an actual client when there is money on the line. My suggestion is to take the strategies you are about to learn and start applying them to your everyday, non-business situations until you reach a level of confidence and competence you feel comfortable applying in actual selling situations.

We already discussed rule number one when it comes to negotiating—sometimes the best deal is the one you *don't* make. Here are the next two *golden rules*—there are two sides to every issue, and *everything* is negotiable.

I realize that every selling and negotiating situation is different, just as the individual participants are different. However, I think you'll see as we progress through this chapter that there are several techniques and strategies you can begin applying (with repetition) on your personal sphere of contacts, then on your professional contacts, to the point where you become a *natural negotiator*, even on a subconscious level, as part of your normal conversation style. I know you've encountered those types of individuals (we all have) where every word that comes out of their mouth seems to have a purpose. They always seem to easily *win friends and influence people* as part of their normal communication style. And yes, we all have our own style—for better or worse. With a few tips and a little practice, you can become an effective and skilled communicator—and fairly quickly.

The real key to negotiating in a professional situation is to make it seem that you are not really negotiating at all, but rather simply having a casual exchange of ideas. You must also realize that each situation and each individual is different. There will, of course, be similar characteristics present in each individual circumstance since you probably sell the same basic product or service over and over again to basically the same consumer base.

Here are a few tips to begin applying your new style of communicating—sorry, *negotiating*.

1. **What is important to you may not be to them: This is where you must put yourself in your prospect's shoes and try to get a feel for** *his* **priorities and major concerns.**

2. **Try not to narrow the negotiations down to just one issue: There are two reasons for this. First, it eliminates the possibility of a "win/win" situation; and second, it leaves little or no room for** *give and take.*

3. **Realize that two parties can see one issue in two entirely different ways. Both sides can be wrong, just as both sides can be right.**

4. **You are negotiating all the time: You just need to start becoming more aware of when and how, so you can begin to direct those** *negotiations* **more in your favor. All you need to do is transfer that comfort and familiarity of your normal and natural personal negotiations to your professional situations in a structured and focused manner.**

The Three Stages of Negotiating

1. **Identify exactly what the other party wants and/or** *requires* **to make the sale.**

2. **Exchange information and objectives.**

3. **Strive for a compromise until the sale is made or the possibility of one is eliminated.**

Whenever you *make* a concession, always *get* a concession in return. This will keep the process flowing and progressing toward the desired outcome. It's also what negotiating is all about—*give and take*. Also always remember to get that return concession *immediately* after making a concession yourself. As the negotiations progress, the significance of your concession will diminish. Strike while the iron is hot!

Whenever possible, choose your own ground. That is why, as a salesperson myself, I always preferred my office's "closing room" as opposed to my prospect's office or home environment. Obviously not every selling situation enables you to bring the prospect back to the office to close the sale, but whenever possible, pick a selling environment of your own choosing. Hopefully, one that's comfortable, familiar, and distraction free.

Always be willing to walk away. Which goes back to what I said earlier; "Sometimes the best deal is the one you *don't* make." Your ability to say *no* is a crucial part of your success and leverage in the negotiation process. If your counterpart knows that you *want* the sale, but don't *need* the sale (your ability to walk away), you are negotiating from a position of strength as opposed to *under the gun*.

Avoid *take it or leave it* ultimatums—unless you mean it. Only use this position as a *last* resort and if you are willing to accept the consequences of them *calling your bluff.*

Stay focused on the *issues* involved and not the personalities. In other words, *don't take it personal*—easier said than done during the heat of negotiations with egos and dollars on the line. The key here is to watch your words as well as your actions. Your body language will convey anger or impatience on your part more so than your words. While you're busy watching *your* body language for signs of anger or impatience, you will also want to watch the body language of your counterpart for those same things. It only takes one side becoming angry or impatient to disrupt the entire negotiating process.

Negotiating Tips and Techniques

The Feel, Felt, Found Technique: Whenever a prospect voices the same concern or objection a *second* time, you must at least address that concern, if not overcome it altogether. This is a great technique for showing your concern and understanding for the prospect's position:

> *"I can appreciate how you **feel**."*
> *"Others have **felt** the same way."*
> *"But what they have **found** is that...."*

With this technique, you show empathy for the prospect's position and let him know he is not alone in that position—others have had the same concern as well. But despite those concerns, the *others* made the purchase and benefited from it. Then you list the benefits of your product or service as they pertain to the prospect's concern or hesitancy.

The Colombo Technique: Those of you familiar with the 1970s television series *Colombo*, will remember Peter Falk's portrayal as a *seemingly* inept and confused detective. Notice I said *seemingly* inept and confused. In reality, the character used that non-threatening, almost incompetent manner to unwittingly gain the upper hand with the suspect as he *negotiated* them into confessing.

At this point, you may be thinking my advice is to go in there, act like a bumbling fool, and hope they give you the sale out of pity. Not at all...however, there are times when a non-threatening, more benign approach to a selling or negotiating situation is the best bet. In fact, the ideal result of negotiating is to convince the buyer it was *his* idea to buy in the first place. By utilizing this technique of *deferring leadership* to the client, he often will lead *himself* right into the sale.

The beauty of Detective Colombo's reserved communication style was that although it appeared to the suspect that *he was* leading or in charge of the conversation, nothing was farther from the truth. Colombo's seemingly haphazard and confused manner often gained information from the suspect he had no intention of divulging...ever, which probably accounts for his 100 percent conviction rate seven seasons in a row.

There's no need to act as if you're the smartest person in the room or appear to know everything.

In fact that's probably the *last* thing you want to do. Remember that the person in charge of the conversation (negotiation) is the one asking the questions. If you already know everything, what questions will you ask to gain control?

There is a big difference between being curious and being ignorant. Colombo often asked his most probative questions almost as an afterthought, usually catching the suspect off guard. The key is to gain specific information by asking general (curious) questions. Try to ask them in a way that makes it appear you just thought of it, like Colombo—almost as an afterthought.

The "Is that the best you can do?" Technique: This technique is common among horse traders and Persian rug salespersons. Unless it's exactly what you want, no negotiator worth his or her salt *ever* takes the first offer. A real savvy negotiator might even *seem* offended by it. Quick rule of thumb: Very seldom is the *first* offer the *best* offer.

Depending on the particular selling or negotiating situation that is presented, your response to any opening offer should always be courteous, respectful, and optimistic. But also reserved in some way. Your prospect may have just *thrown out* the first offer to see what your reaction to it would be. If you react with a grimace or other mannerism that signals some form of disappointment or reservation on your part, the prospect will understand that more "give" needs to take place on their part before any "take" can occur on yours.

Little Yes Now, Big Yes Later Technique: This is a pretty basic selling and negotiating principle. As we discussed in the previous chapter, getting incremental concessions from the client in the form of saying *yes* to minor or "little" issues early in the process makes it that much easier to get the "big" *yes* out of them on the main points. If you are dealing with significant or costly items or services that require a more detailed selling process to take place, then a quick jump off the deep end by asking the prospect if he wants to buy right off the bat may not be the most effective strategy.

Start by finding small agreeable points the prospect can commit to, and then gradually raise the stakes until you and the client have reached a level of comfort and rapport necessary to begin engaging in the major topics and issues.

The Higher Authority Technique: This was made famous by used car salespersons everywhere. Come on, we all know there's no mysterious unseen "sales manager" locked away upstairs whose job it is to grind every penny out of us before giving into the desperate pleas of the salesperson to *give these poor folks a break*…just this once! Why do they always try to pull that one? Because it works!

If possible, don't be afraid to lay the *bad guy* label squarely where it belongs—on the imaginary sales manager upstairs who never approves anything. The key to this deferred authority technique is that it enables the salesperson to remain a neutral, almost *allied* participant in the negotiations. It almost becomes a "them versus us" mentality. "Them" of course being the higher authority, and "us" being you and the other party working *together* as a *team*—instead of against each other. I've been a used car salesperson and actually had clients thank me for talking the "sales manager" (another salesperson with no customer at the time) into taking their offer.

It was quite a routine. I'd emerge from heated negotiations with the sales manager (or if a lack thereof, the snack machine) with my hair mussed up, necktie slightly undone and sometimes for good effect, wiping the sweat off my brow. I'd actually have an almost pained and exhausted expression on my face (for additional good effect). I'll never forget the look of anticipation on the customers' faces as I emerged with *the good news*. I also never forget the looks of gratitude for my hard work in talking the manager into letting them buy.

The Take Away Technique: This is also known as The Fear of Loss Technique. TV advertisers use this technique on us all the time—"Act now while supplies last." The meaning is obvious; if we do not buy "now," the chance to buy later may be *taken away* or *lost* because supplies may not last.

If you are dealing with a customer that is exhibiting a desire to make the purchase but is showing minor signs of hesitancy, the *Take Away Technique* is designed to create a sense of urgency for the buyer to *act now* or possibly lose the chance to act *ever*. You know the old adage that we never appreciate what we have until we lose it. The fear of loss concept gets the prospect to at least consider, for a second, the negative consequences of losing the opportunity to make the purchase while at the same time appreciating the opportunity to make the purchase now…while there's still time.

Here's a personal example of how I have used this technique on my own clients. I offered a training program to the real estate industry with the same name as this book—*SELL LIKE CRAZY.* Although I consider the program an exceptional opportunity for realty organizations, on occasion it does take some *selling* on the part of myself or one of my program directors to sell the program to certain brokers. When I or one of my program directors encounter a particular broker or organization that we'd like to work with and that has a desire or need for our program, but is a little hesitant to make the commitment at that time, we will use this variation of the Take Away Technique:

"You might be right; maybe this *isn't* the right time or the right program for your company." Ninety percent of the time, the client will disagree with that assessment and go ahead and retain our services, right then and there. Nobody likes to feel like he is not *wanted* or qualified for something.

The Reduce to the Ridiculous Technique: This is also known as divide and minimize. When a prospect conveys what he *believes* is a major concern, but you believe is not, there is a way to address the issue that diminishes it while not dismissing it, kind of like getting the customer to focus on each tree individually as opposed to the forest as a whole.

Once the prospect has expressed a concern, you must try your best to take the big picture, so to speak, and break it down into a series of smaller pictures the customer is more easily able to digest. That is the difference between how we make our credit card *purchases* and how we make our credit card *payments*. Face it; the only way most of us will go out and spend thousands of dollars on a single purchase is because of our ability to see that large purchase as just a series of smaller purchases over time. In our minds, we are not spending three grand all at once (even though we are); we are spending only a few hundred a month. Once the credit card companies started reducing our large purchases to ridiculous small payments, not only did consumers becoming willing to pay triple the price for something (over time with interest), credit cards have become a preferred method of purchase among consumers worldwide.

Salespeople who deal with higher priced products and services must become skilled at taking the customer's focus off the price (major con-cern) and redirecting it more toward the benefits of owning the product over time as opposed to paying for it today.

Car salespeople encounter this all the time, espe-cially when they try to add on all those expen-sive little extras—usually increasing the cost of the vehicle significantly. Much like buying a product with a credit card significantly increases its cost, because of interest and other fees. We are willing to make that big purchase if we can be shown that it is in fact nothing more than a series of small purchases.

So how does a car salesperson get a buyer to pay a thousand dollars more for a car because it comes with a better sound system? By showing the buyer the better sound system does *not* cost an additional thousand dollars. It only costs elev-en cents a day over the life of the loan. The same technique is used by real estate professionals when encountering purchase prices in the hundreds of thousands of dollars—enter financing. That seem-ingly insurmountable two hundred thousand dol-lar price tag (problem) is now a manageable two thousand per month (no problem).

The Over-Shoot Technique: This technique is of course the essence of negotiating. It's simply a matter of asking for more than you want and bar-gaining downward from there to an acceptable level. The key here is not to start so high that it offends your counterpart, but also not so low that it offends you.

This is also the flip side of what we discussed earlier about not accepting the first offer because it's probably not the best offer you can obtain. This technique is based on *your* first offer not being the best either.

Now that we have discussed some proven and successful negotiating techniques, let's take a look at the different personality types you will be applying those techniques on and how best to handle each one.

The Four Personality Types
1. EXTROVERT:

> *Characteristics*
> Avoids details
> Likes to get excited
> Take charge mentality
> Firm handshake
> Gives their name easily
> Plenty of eye-to-eye contact when conversing
> Makes decisions quickly
> Friendly and open manner
> Warm greeter
> Speaks easily regarding personal matters
> Personable but assertive
> Avoids follow up

How to Handle

Speak and gesture in an enthusiastic manner.

Emphasize results and benefits.

Ask for and expect a quick decision.

Use stories and anecdotes during presentation.

Make ultimate goal a win/win situation.

2. PRAGMATIC:

Characteristics

All business, no-nonsense demeanor

Bottom line, get to the point attitude

Decides on logic

Take charge mentality

Firm handshake

Volunteers information easily

Maintains eye contact when conversing

Decides quickly

Avoids small talk

Less accessible

Formal dresser

Does not like or respond well to visuals

How to Handle

Focus presentation to their needs and what's in it for them.

Avoid informal or small talk.

Don't overload with details or information.

Stick to the main points and pertinent facts.

Keep conversations mostly professional in content.

Do not attempt to dominate the conversation. Defer to prospects. They often exhibit a street fighter negotiating style—main goal to win at all cost. Always let them *believe* they have won.

3. AMIABLE:

Characteristics
Never pushy, especially when it comes to opinions and views
Warm and friendly personality
Maintains social barriers when conversing with strangers
Item and "thing" oriented as opposed to a people person
Usually not in upper management position
Finds it difficult to say "no"
Hates change and unfamiliarity

How to Handle
Talk and gesture slowly.
Keep conversation neutral.
Validate him as a person as well as a client by complimenting him on a personal issue.
Never come across as pushy or demanding, or trying to pressure him.
Focus on getting him to like and trust *you* more than on what you're selling.
Spend a lot of time on the rapport building stage before moving on to the actual selling and closing processes.

Engage him in a *give and take* style of conversation. Your main goal is that *everyone* is happy. Declare the sale a win/win!

4. ANALYTICAL:

Characteristics
Decides on logic
Less likely to push their views on others
Details oriented
Need to know "how" more than "what"
Hates change
Professor Gadget personality type
Likes visuals and hands on "stuff"
Information and facts oriented

How to Handle
Make sure all aspects of your conversation and presentation are accurate.
Give plenty of details and data.
Use charts and visual aids.
Ask plenty of questions.
Avoid a pushy manner.
Their main goal is less to win than it is to maintain an orderly negotiating session.

Naturally, not every prospect you meet will fit neatly into one of these four categories, but if you take a closer look at those you come into contact with, I believe you will find that many share the common characteristics of whatever group they fall into.

As an exercise, select ten people from your personal and professional circles and try to accurately divide them into one of the four groups by identifying their personality characteristics. Then engage them in a conversation using the *how to handle* techniques described for each type, as well as other techniques learned from this chapter and the chapter on Effective Communication.

Before moving on to the next chapter let me give the final four keys to successful negotiating: Honesty, Information, Timing, Technique.

The real key for you is to develop your own techniques, strategies, and style using these principles. Remember that the real objective of all selling negotiations is to attain a win/win situation for *all* parties. Therefore, regardless of the outcome, *never* gloat and *always* remember to congratulate your opponent for a game well played.

"Be Prepared!"

THE BOY SCOUTS MOTTO

CHAPTER 24: CLOSING THE SALE

$

"Just Do It!"   RUNNING SHOE AD

What you are going to learn in this chapter are several effective closing techniques and specific dialogue that, if done properly, can actually make asking for the sale the easiest part of your presentation. Unfortunately, for most salespeople, closing for the sale is often the hardest part.

We have discussed the importance of believing in your particular product or service and that it indeed benefits those who purchase and use it. It's twice as hard to sell something that you are not first sold on yourself. Enthusiasm is contagious; if you are excited about what you are selling, it's that much easier to get others excited as well.

You must believe that you are acting in the best interest of the client when you close for the sale. You must believe that you are even doing him a disservice by not asking him to buy. The way you believe those things is by first believing in yourself and what you are selling. That's the basis for an easy and comfortable closing process—*belief*.

Let me give you a personal example of how my lack of confidence (belief in myself) as a newly licensed realtor may have cost some of my clients a shot at the American dream. When I first entered the field of real estate sales, I lacked the same thing every new agent lacked: confidence. It was not so much a lack of confidence in my product, which happened to be Southern California real estate in the 1980s—enough said—but more from a lack of confidence in *myself* and my abilities as a sales agent, especially involving such high-ticket items like houses and development property. Needless to say, because of my lack of confidence, my *hard sell* left a lot to be desired. Sometimes my confidence was so low that I wouldn't even ask the buyers if they were interested in making an offer on any of the homes I would show them. I assumed because they didn't outright indicate they wanted to buy the house that they didn't—and who was I to ask them? After all, I was just their *realtor*!

My hesitancy and lack of confidence kept me from pressing them to make an offer on a home I knew was perfect for them. I didn't have the *courage* because I didn't have the *confidence*. Now here's the sad part. Some of those people who trusted me to do my job are still renting because I didn't have the guts at least to *ask* them to buy. The houses I didn't have the courage to "hard sell" at the time are now selling for ten times what they were selling for back then. That tough decision I failed to help those clients make would have been, could have been, and should have been one of the most profitable investments of their entire lives. I think about those clients from time to time.

Here is a list of my all-time favorite closing techniques.

Phil's Favorite Closes

Ask: Believe me; the buyer knows what you want. Asking him to buy what you are selling isn't going to be a surprise to anyone. Stop pretending that you and the buyer are just two ships passing in the night and, somehow when it's all over, a sale will have taken place. Later in the chapter, we will discuss specific dialogues for *asking* for the sale.

The Assumptive Close: This close is usually reserved for the bravest of the brave. Which of course is *you*. Right? The *assumptive close* is based on the "assumption" that since the prospect has not actually said "no," the only option left is "yes." Therefore, your presentation and closing process are given with the attitude or the *assumption* that the sale has, for all intents and purposes, already been made. Your actions and words must reflect this assumption. "Will you buy?" is not an assumptive close. "When can we arrange delivery?" is an example of "assuming" the sale has been made and now it's just a matter of working out the details.

Some prospects simply cannot bring themselves to say the word "yes," especially among higher obligation purchases. That's where the assumptive close comes in. You are basically saying "yes" for them.

Most closes come at the end of the selling and presenting process. However, the assumptive close actually takes place *during* the sales presentation. Your attitude and dialogue follow a pattern that directs the prospect to the point of the sale. So actually, your entire sales presentation is the *assumptive close*. The end of the presentation is simply a matter of asking for his approval or handing him the pen and directing his signature.

The Minor Agreement Close: The concept here is to deliver during your presentation a series of smaller or "little" closes, which gradually lead the prospect and the salesperson to the big yes. Which is of course is the response to, "Will you buy?"

As any good lawyer will tell you, never ask a question you don't already know the answer to. To take it a step further, not only ask a question you already know the answer to, but also make sure it's the answer you want to hear—which is easier to do because *you* are structuring the questions.

That is why I recommend a series of simple and obvious questions, at least initially, that will elicit from the prospect any kind of positive affirmation. Once the prospect gets used to saying "no" to the little things, it's not that hard for him to deal you the big "no."

The "While We're At It" Close, or if you prefer, *"The Close after the Close" Close*: Many selling situations offer the opportunity of *buying up* or *add-on* products and services. Let us again use the purchase of a vehicle as the example. Once the prospect has been sold on making the purchase, now he must be sold on making the purchases that go with the purchase, so to speak. No self respecting car dealer is going to let you off the lot with just the car. There are always those little extras you'll need to enhance your driving experience.

There's a reason I call this the "while we're at it" close, because that is your close—"*While we're at it*, how about some new tires, chrome rims…." This concept is the exact opposite of the *minor agreement* close. In this instance, you first get the "big" yes out of the way, and then begin working on those little ones. The best way to get a commitment on the little yes is to link them to the prospect's commitment to the big yes. You do this by tying the two together with the verbiage "while we're at it." While we're at what? While we're at the point where you are buying what I'm selling! And since you're in the mood to buy….

The Alternate of Choice Close: This is sometimes referred to as the *"this or that"* close. It is basically an extension of the *assumptive close* to the point where you are *assuming* the prospect is going to make the purchase. However, under this scenario, your closing technique is getting the prospect to commit to "which one" he is going to buy, as opposed to *if* he will buy at all. You have taken the buying options of "yes" or "no" and converted them into "which one." In the first case, you have a 50 percent chance of getting the sale from the "yes or no" closing technique. With the alternate of choice close, it's a win/win situation for you. As I detail in the following chapter on Quality Service, it should also be a winning situation for the client as well. Never forget, it may take several closes before the prospect says yes, so hang in there.

When it comes to giving the prospect an alternate choice between two items make sure both choices are designed to elicit a positive response that direct the process to the desired conclusion: the sale.

The Conditional or "Subject to" Close: This closing technique is exactly what the title implies. It is a commitment from the client to buy on the "condition" or "subject to" a certain condition being met or circumstance occurring. If there is indeed a condition of the sale then you must identify and isolate it as soon as possible, especially if it's a condition that cannot be met.

The key is to get the prospect to commit to the purchase without him actually realizing he has agreed to buy...once the condition has been met. You are using the very same reason the buyer gives why he can't buy right now (or at all), and turning it into a commitment to buy later…once the condition has been met.

There are different definitions of the word "later." If you're a salesperson—it means *never*.

Sometimes you are going to be hit with real conditions that indeed will prevent the prospect from buying now or possibly ever. But the majority of those so called conditions are really only "stalls" or delaying tactics on the part of the buyer to delay a commitment until a retreat or *not now* plan can be formulated. With that in mind a "yes" is anything but a direct "no," and if it's not a direct "yes" then it's probably a stall or delaying tactic—so keep closing for the sale. Don't let them off the hook with only a stall. If all else fails in getting them to make the purchase right then and there, try converting their stall to a delayed commitment to buy.

All a hesitant prospect is usually looking for is a way to get themselves not so much out of the sale, but more out of having to make a commitment to purchase at that moment. But like I said, if all else fails, go ahead and give it to him, but not without first getting a commitment *now* to buy *later*.

The Recommend Close: This close is never to be used lightly or without careful consideration of the client's best interests. As an ethical salesperson, you should never recommend anything to anyone you do not sincerely believe in yourself, or believe it will benefit the client. There are too many valuable and legitimate services and products out there to sell without lowering yourself to the level of recommending something not worthy of recommendation.

Once you have gathered as many facts as possible and/or necessary about the client and his particular needs and wants, and you legitimately feel the client can and will benefit from what you are offering, then by all means make the recommendation to purchase. After all, if you can't recommend what you're selling how can you recommend that someone buy it? Besides—you'll sleep better at night.

When I reached the point in my presentation where the prospect was ready to buy but for some reason needed that extra little "push," I would take the responsibility of suggesting he make the purchase. I know that seems kind of obvious—a salesperson recommending a prospect buy the product, but that is why I say "after" you have gathered as much information as needed or possible. *Then* make a credible recommendation based on the facts about the client and not just the desire to make the sale at any cost.

"Based on what you've told me, I recommend you go ahead and make the purchase."

The Buy or Die/Now or Never Close: Every salesperson knows the frustration of trying to convert prospects who just will not get off the fence. Not only are they wasting your time, they are allowing you to waste *their* time as well. As a salesperson myself, I never had the patience to play that game…for very long that is. I would let them get their traditional stalls, objections, and conditions out of the way—then I'd cut quickly to the chase.

The direct close is best done *directly*. "I've given you all the information I can to help you make an informed decision. Now it's up to you…are you ready to buy?" Then shut up and wait for them to give a yes or no answer! Hang in there; some people take a little time to make decisions. I've sat there for what seemed like two minutes in silence staring at a prospect, not knowing if he heard me, was thinking about it, or perhaps misunderstood me. But sooner or later, the head started to nod and the lips started to move, and more often than not, I got my "yes."

The Shut Up Close: Yep, you guessed it; once you ask *any* closing question—especially the *big* closing question—*shut up* and don't say anything until they say something back! Remember, maybe they're thinking about it? Either way, here is the basic rule of thumb when it comes to the "shut up" close: The first person to talk loses the staring contest and maybe the sale as well.

The "If I Could…. Would You…?" Close: This was usually the first hard close I used on my clients. It's a variation of the *conditional close*. All you do is take whatever objection or stall the prospect has given as to why he *believes* he can't buy or buy right now, then ask him directly that if you can meet that condition, then would he buy? Keep in mind, the problem you offer to solve must be solvable in the first place. If not, then you have a legitimate *condition* of the sale.

The Take Away Close: Here is not only a basic rule of selling—but also of life in general. The fear of loss is a greater motivator than the opportunity for gain. Did you get that? Most people will fight harder to keep what they have than they will to gain something new. Even though the prospect hasn't *gained* what you are selling yet (hence the need for a close), if properly communicated to him, he will fight to "keep" the opportunity to buy, but only if he senses the "loss" of that opportunity is at hand. This particular close is almost a bluff of sorts on your part. So make it subtle and not too restrictive. In other words, leave yourself a way out of this close in case the prospect calls your bluff.

If the prospect will not commit to purchase *right now*, he may lose the opportunity to buy later, or at all. Don't be afraid to let him know this. Those take-away techniques are used on us all the time—*only the first five hundred callers qualify; Limited time offer*!

At which point, we immediately grab the phone and *call now while operators are standing by*, only to wait on hold for an hour or so in the mere hope that our once in a lifetime opportunity to take advantage of that limited time only offer hasn't been *taken away*. Homes all across the country are filled with useless junk because a TV commercial instilled in the viewer a "fear of loss" to the point where that viewer not only made a commitment to buy but also acted on that commitment *right now*. And it all happened in less than thirty seconds.

Using the *take away* close is a great study in human nature and behavior. Individually consumers are all different, but collectively they're all the same.

The "What Would it Take?" Close: This is a great close to use on prospects who seem "stuck on the fence." After you have given them all the benefits of making the purchase, effectively handled their objections, asked for the sale (at least three times), you still may have a case of indecision or hesitancy on the part of the prospect. That is when you give them, "What would it take for you to make the purchase right now?" Then of course *shut up* until they tell you.

If the prospect responds with something like, "It would take winning the lottery for me to afford the purchase," then you have a "condition" on your hands and not an objection or a stall. The key behind this close is to get the prospect to state verbally exactly what has to happen in order for him to buy. If it's something you can provide or do for him, then it's just a matter of isolating the objection, confirming the objection as the *only* reason, and then overcoming it.

Always be sure to follow up the buyers condition(s) with, "So what you're saying is, if I can (overcome the objection) then you are ready to buy today?" If they say, "yes" then now you know exactly what it's going to take to get them to buy. Then it becomes simply a matter of meeting the condition if possible. Remember, sometimes the best deal is the one you *don't* make. You will also have to decide if the condition is worth your time or effort to make the sale. Selling is still a numbers game and this particular close is designed to speed up the closing process or quickly eliminate the prospect.

The Reduce to the Ridiculous Close: You may recall we discussed the application of this technique in the chapter on negotiating. We used sellers of higher-end purchases such as vehicles and real estate and how those sales professionals took a large single sum dollar amount and "reduced" it to a series of smaller payments over time.

If the overall price for your product or service or some other aspect of purchase is significant enough to be an issue to some of your customers, then find a way to take the entirety of the purchase price or the issue and break it down into smaller components, such as individual payments, the real cost of ownership over time, or big benefits for a small price. The key is to make major issues appear smaller when put into the proper context.

The Initial Shock Close: I once had the pleasure of meeting the little girl who held the record for selling the most boxes of cookies door-to-door for her particular school's fund raising drive. I also had the very enlightening experience of learning her secret. She would walk up to a potential customer and ask him if he would like to buy some cookies? Invariably he would ask, "How much?" at which point she would reply, "Forty-five dollars a case." Naturally, the prospect would say he had no interest in purchasing an entire case of cookies, especially for $45. At which point she would let him off the hook; "Then would you at least buy one box for three dollars?"

When it comes to using the "initial shock" close, do not be afraid to hit them with the worst case first, or in her case—the *entire* case.

The Ben Franklin Balance Sheet Close: This is a close that relies just as much on its *visual* aspect as it does *verbal.* When you give the prospect all the advantages of making the purchase and he responds with all the *disadvantages* of making it, it's time to get out the *Ben Franklin Balance Sheet* and compare notes.

All you need is a piece of paper and pen or pencil. Draw a line down the middle of the paper making two columns. At the top of one column, draw a "plus" sign and at the top of the other column, draw a "minus" sign. Under the plus sign, list all the benefits to the client if he makes the purchase, and under the column with the minus sign list all the negatives the client has given you. Remember, when it comes to negatives and positives, sometimes *quality* outweighs *quantity*. What I mean by this is, do not get intimidated if the minus column has more disadvantages listed than the plus column has advantages. Perhaps the numerically superior negatives are outweighed by one or two key positives. If you have a product or service that truly is a benefit to the customer, then you should never be afraid to put it to this test.

The "Try It—You'll Like It" Close: We've all heard the familiar, *"Aw, go on...you only live once,"* from those smooth talking salespeople. Don't be afraid to get a little "smooth" yourself. If you truly believe the client is going to benefit or "like" what you're selling, you shouldn't be afraid to throw in a little personal endorsement.

Just keep it simple with no unrealistic promises attached. *Try it you'll like it* is enough, as opposed to "If you buy this you'll love it! I swear." I also suggest throwing this at the prospect in *an off the cuff* or informal manner, almost as an afterthought and never as the initial close. This is more of a "Hail Mary" type of closing technique when you're running out of time and nothing else has gotten the prospect to commit.

The "Any Questions?" Close:
Once you have given your sales presentation, extolled all the benefits, minimized the clients perceived as well as real negatives, and isolated and overcame their objections, it is now time to wrap up the sale. Here's how: "Any questions?" if they say "no," then congratulations you have a sale.

> **"One hundred percent of the shots you don't take don't go in."**
>
> WAYNE GRETZKY

SECTION 5: The Sales Professional

"There is only one boss. The customer. And he can fire everybody in the company from the Chairman on down, simply by spending his money elsewhere."

SAM WALTON

CHAPTER 25: QUALITY SERVICE

*P*eople don't care how much you know until they know how much you care. The best way to show your clients that you care is by dealing with them and their needs in an honest and ethical manner. The next step, of course, is doing everything possible to offer your clients more and better service than they can obtain elsewhere. Offering *more and better* will be an ongoing, ever increasing endeavor on your part.

When it came to customer service and satisfaction in my career as a salesperson, I had one philosophy. It was not my goal to satisfy my customers; it was to *amaze* them! You would be surprised at how little it took on my part to do just that. Sometimes it's just as simple as thanking them for their business or letting them know you appreciate the opportunity to be of service. Other times it's a matter of having a genuine concern for the needs and wants of your clients when a problem arises. In my opinion, 90 percent of customer dissatisfaction could be solved with the following two phrases: "Thank you" and "I'm sorry." You can't beat the price of that investment.

The place to begin your quest for better serving of your clients is first to realize the *importance* of better serving your clients. If you are in the business of selling, then you are in a *service* industry. More service means more business; it's that simple. In fact, businesses who list quality service and control programs as a top priority report an average of 30 percent more sales volume compared to other operations in the same industry who pay little or no attention to such programs. So, if you're still not sold on the concept of giving your clients that little extra they deserve and sometimes expect, don't worry; sooner or later you will become a believer, right about the time you see those dissatisfied customers showing up at your competitor's door.

When it comes to selling anything, whether it's you, your organization, service or product, the most valuable commodity you have is your *reputation*.

The field of sales involves more than just supply and demand. It involves your relationship with your buying public and, just as importantly, their relationship with you. That means in addition to selling your particular product or service you are also in the business of selling your customers on you, your organization's good reputation, the confidence that you or your product will do what the customer needs, and so on. If you think a creative sales pitch is going to do all that for you, think again.

If that were the case, all that would be needed for a successful quality service program would be a *"New and Improved"* label slapped on the box every so often along with the claim *"We're number 1, again."* I believe such superficial *white-washings* are a thing of the past, especially thanks to the Internet, where research on any company or product is just a click away.

Remember the difference between reality and *perceived* reality when it comes to selling? What the consumer *believes* to be true about you and the product or service you are trying to sell is, in his mind, "the truth," even if what he believes is completely false. That is why it is so important to establish your reputation among consumers before they establish it for themselves.

I'm sorry to say many companies' version of providing quality care and service to their customers is simply putting a new label on the old package. And just as sorry, I guess, is the fact that more often than not it works.

Here is a personal example of the difference between reality and perceived reality. One day as the manager of a real estate office in Southern California, I received a call from a disgruntled client who had their house listed for sale with our company. On this particular day, she was looking to change that and cancel her listing agreement.

When I asked her what the reason for her displeasure was, she told me that despite her agents promise to "stay in touch on a regular basis," the agent had done anything but that. In fact, she said her agent "only calls me once a week!" On my oath to rectify the situation to the satisfaction of the client, she agreed to keep her home listed with our company. The next thing I did was call that agent into my office and explain the situation and the client's complaint of "not staying in touch on a regular basis." That agent's response was one of the most insightful experiences I have ever had regarding customer relations. She said, "But Phil, I call her once a week, I swear!" There is no reality—only *perceived* reality.

Both the salesperson and the client had the same reality—weekly contact. What differed was their *perception* of that so called same reality. So who was right? I'll give you a hint; the customer is *always* right. That's where an effective program of quality customer care and service comes in. It not only gets you out of trouble, very often, it keeps you out of it in the first place.

Let me ask you this. Do diners want more than a meal? Do hotel guests want more than a room? Do people who purchase automobiles want more than a car? Of course they do! That is how a business grows and prospers—through satisfied customers. Satisfied customers turn into loyal customers, and loyal satisfied customers not only come back, they often bring their friends back with them. That is the strongest argument I can make for making and keeping your customers happy.

Quality Service Chain Reaction

1. **Quality service leads to customer satisfaction.**

2. **Customer satisfaction leads to customer loyalty.**

3. **Customer loyalty leads to referrals and recommendations.**

4. **Referrals and recommendations leads to new customers.**

5. **New customers lead to quality service, and so on...**

Satisfied customers not only come back, they often come back with other buyers.

Unfortunately, there's only really two times in the history of a sale when you even know you have a client. First is at the time of purchase, and the other is when there's a problem with that purchase.

The following are the results of an extensive survey conducted by my organization among the top rated customer satisfaction and service leaders in the sales industry. We found they shared the following common beliefs.

1. **Quality service is profitable**

2. **Customer satisfaction is their top priority.**

3. **Satisfied customers not only provide repeat business, but also are responsible for a majority of new customer referrals.**

4. **Companies with high customer service and satisfaction ratings are able to charge an additional 7 to 10 percent more for their goods and services.**

5. **Quality service leaders not only listen to their customers and employees, but also implement their suggestions.**

6. **Quality service leaders respond quickly, positively, and courteously to complaints.**

7. **Quality service organizations emphasize training and coaching programs.**

8. **Quality service companies have nearly double the retention rate of their customers and employees over competitors with no such programs.**

The first place to start implementing your own quality service program is with a clear awareness of what a successful customer care and service program would mean to your particular situation. Would it mean more productivity or sales? Would it mean a more pleasant and productive office or sales environment? Would it mean more referrals and re-sells? I hope all of the above, but whatever your individual situation, try to define exactly what the benefits of your efforts would be. Seeing those benefits in writing will make them seem more real and will help motivate you to implement them.

The next step is to start *listening*. Listen to your clients. Listen to your employees. Listen to the cleaning crew if necessary. Listen to anyone related to your business activities that might be able to provide unique insight or help identify a problem (or solution) you may not even be aware exists.

The third step in creating your quality service program is to take the results and information gathered from your research to identify which aspects you *will* do (not just *can* do) and should do, to better serve your customers and market. You should also set realistic time frames for their implementation.

The forth step is of course to begin implementing your program's plan of action. Just remember, good reputations take a lot longer to develop and establish than bad reputations do—so don't get impatient.

You don't necessarily have to be more successful or even better at satisfying your customers than your competition, although that would be a great advantage. Sometimes being perceived as just *trying harder* than your competitors is enough. In fact, Avis Car Rental has become a powerhouse based on this concept. Remember their TV commercials? "We're number *two*…which means we try harder."

It always seems nobody cares or even notices when you do something right. But one small slip up and the whole world knows and cares about it. As I said earlier, if you are in the sales business, then you are in the *service* business, and if you are in the service business, you are going to encounter problems with some of your customers. So I recommend having a pre-established plan of action already in place to deal with those problems as they occur, or even better, *before* they occur (preventative).

When a Problem Occurs

1. **Stay calm, even when no one else is.**

2. **Do not take it personally—ever! It's only business.**

3. **Do not interrupt a customer in mid complaint. Hear him out entirely.**

4. **Do not let the customer provoke you. For some it's the only goal.**

5. **Emphasize you and your company's concern for a customer's problem and its solution.**

6. **Be patient.**

7. **Be tactful.**

8. **Let the customer know his problem is important to you personally.**

9. **If you made a mistake, admit it.**

10. **Never argue or rise to their level of anger.**

11. **Speak in a slow, clear, and calm manner.**

12. **Ask your customer what you can do** *right now* **to make him feel good about this situation.**

13. **Do it if possible, if not, at least do something to make him feel better.**

The second important area to focus on is something I immediately implement with any new company I work with. I call it our *Quality Service Pledge*. I have the company put in writing their quality service objectives and commitments, along with certain promises and goals they have regarding their customers' satisfaction. We then have each member of the organization, especially the sales representatives who deal directly with the buying public, sign the pledge. Every customer or prospect is given a copy of the pledge to show, in writing, the company's commitment (pledge) to quality customer service.

Here are some tips for establishing your own Quality Service Pledge:

1. **Create a service statement or oath that clearly states your primary goal, such as Federal Express'** *– Absolutely, positively over night*; **or Dominoes Pizza** *– Delivered to you in 30 minutes or it's free*; **or Lens Crafters** *– Custom made eyeglasses in about an hour.* **Find a way to say, in as few words as possible, exactly what you, your company, and what you provide stand for** *and how it benefits the customer.*

2. **Direct your efforts toward and include items that are most important to your customers. If you want to know what is most important to your customers, just ask them.**

3. **Create a program that clearly separates you from your competitors.**

4. **Develop a program that your staff (the ultimate implementers of the program) believe in and will enthusiastically support.**

5. **Choose objectives that you can and will complete. The best plan is always the one that gets done.**

I hope I provided you a little insight into the importance of taking care of and providing for your customers in a way they notice and appreciate. If you always take care of your customers, they will always take care of you. The best way to "take care" of your customers is to always provide a level of service, care, and support to the point where they no longer see you as a salesperson but more like a friend in the business.

RULE #1: *If we don't take care of the customer...somebody else will.*

The reason that most salespeople don't prospect for clients as effectively as they could is simply because most salespeople have never learned or been taught how to effectively prospect. For the most part, it's simply a lack of training and/or experience. Prospecting, just like selling, is a process that can be learned and mastered. Keep in mind what I said earlier about the difference between experience versus education—you can't learn skill in a classroom or from a book. You can acquire knowledge in the classroom, but you can only gain skill and experience in the field.

So, will more experience in the field make you more effective at prospecting? I'll answer that question this way; practice does not make perfect—*prefect* practice makes perfect. The only way you can effectively prospect in your field is to first learn how to effectively prospect in the classroom—or in this case from a book.

Knowledge without application is *worse* than worthless. Sadly, many salespeople are hesitant to go out in the field and actually begin applying what they perceive as "limited" knowledge, until they feel they have learned enough to feel comfortable enough to face the buying public. Remember the getting ready to get ready syndrome?

Having a case of the getting ready to get ready syndrome can get expensive; it did for me. I was selling Southern California real estate at the time with commission checks representing thousands of dollars a pop. I had to make sure I had every sales tool on the market and attended every training class and seminar—at least twice! I never left the office or made a call until I was certain I had enough knowledge and tools to cover every conceivable selling situation I could possibly encounter, which led to four months without a sale, an empty bank account, tools and training I wasn't using, as well as the need to go out and find a real job.

Eventually, I realized the fact I would never know *everything* there was to know about selling. Besides, even if I could learn everything, by the time I did, most of it would have changed anyway. So I bit the bullet, so to speak, and went out and at least gave it a try. The third door I knocked on became my first listing.

I am not suggesting you just charge right out there and wing it with insufficient training, tools, or confidence. What I am saying is at least take a closer look at what you *believe* to be shortcomings in your skill, knowledge, or level of confidence. Are they indeed the barriers you've made them out to be, or more like self-made safety nets between you and rejection?

If there are indeed real limitations or deficiencies when it comes to your selling skills or tools, then I would recommend taking steps to overcome those limitations immediately—time is money, or in this case…money lost. But in the mean time, do your best to operate successfully within those soon to disappear limitations. Let me give you a good example of what I mean.

As any real estate agent will tell you, the most difficult seller to bag is the *For Sale By Owner*. None but the brave and highly skilled agents need apply.

So how does a brand new real estate agent with limited confidence, skill, and knowledge go after the *hardest of the hard* prospects? By learning to operate within those limitations until I could expand beyond them with increased skill and knowledge. Here's how I did it.

Most For Sale by Owners (FSBOs) would immediately be bombarded with calls and visits from local realtors the minute their ad was published or the for sale sign was put in the front yard. As a feeble deflection method, many would add the phrase "No Agents!" to their ads and signs. Those are the ones I would purposely seek out. I'd walk right up and knock on the door with a copy of their ad in my hand, and ask for the opportunity to present my services. Of course, most times this was met with, "What are you, an idiot? The ad says NO AGENTS!" In which I would reply, "That's why I'm here; according to my Broker, I'm the closest thing to *NO AGENT.*"

More often than not, my remark was met with laughter…and sometimes, "That was pretty good," which was usually followed by, "Okay, come on in and let's see what you've got." My ratio of FSBO contacts to actual listings was the highest in the history of my company, all before my first full year as an agent.

There are some basic rules that apply to most prospecting situations, regardless of your level of skill or knowledge, or lack thereof. The first being *activity creates productivity.* In other words, do-ing *something* is better than doing *nothing,* even if that *something* is done within the limitations of an inexperienced salesperson. I have seen geniuses just sit there at their desks and go broke doing *nothing!* Usually this was because they couldn't do *everything*—so they didn't do *anything,* except of course attend more seminars, read more books, and maybe get their business cards laminated. I have always found that prospecting is a lot like bathing; if you don't do it on a regular basis, pretty soon you stink.

Let me share with you what I believe is a cure for most difficult prospecting situations as well as any limitations you feel you may be suffering from, particularly in the areas of experience, skill, or knowledge: *consistency*. As human beings, we possess this remarkable ability to adjust to just about any circumstance, no matter how unpleasant, if exposed to it long enough or on a regular basis. You can literally prospect your way out of prospecting anxiety—and get paid to do it

Here's the importance of having a consistent pattern to your prospecting efforts. For most salespeople, the mere thought of having to go out and face rejection and failure on a regular basis often becomes a huge, sometimes insurmountable barrier, especially for the newer associates. To bring the level of anxiety, fear, hesitation, and so on, down to a manageable level, try to make your prospecting efforts as routine or consistent as possible. We often grow immune to the negativity of certain situations simply because we encounter them on a regular enough basis.

First, begin by becoming consistent in *when* you prospect. Utilize "Prime Times" (discussed later) and dedicate even a small block of your work schedule to prospecting on as regular and consistent a basis as your schedule permits. Trust me, within a week or so of consistently and regular prospecting, you will begin to see positive results, almost immediately.

Another important part of taking the sting out of prospecting is to exercise commitment. Prospecting is a mental game but it's still a *numbers* game. So be sure to make a commitment at least to conduct a level of activity that will ensure the desired level of *productivity*. In other words, do enough prospecting to get enough sales to reach the goals you listed in the earlier chapter. After a while, you will have an idea of how many times you have to *ask* for business to get business.

Here's a trick I used on brand new associates when it came to prospecting door-to-door or over the phone. Some salespeople still viewed even a small amount of prospecting as too much—despite their income goals to the contrary. So I would say, "Today just go out in the field and knock on *one* door only, or only make *one* call; then you're done for the day. How's that"? They would always say, "Well of course I can do *that*."

The trick was not getting them to make the fifty calls; it was getting them to pick up the phone in the first place. It wasn't making them knock one hundred doors; it was getting them out of the car. The important thing was that I got them to make a *commitment*. More importantly, it was a commitment I and they knew they could and would keep. And that's the key to any commitment—focus more on what you *will* do rather than on what you can or should do.

Here's something fascinating that almost always happened when that salesperson went out to knock on only that one door or make only that one call. They usually came back having knocked on another ninety-nine doors or made the rest of the forty-nine calls. The key was to get them in the saddle and let them make the decision to go for a ride on their own.

Another way to make prospecting a little easier is to get a few notches on your gun belt as quickly as possible. Nothing breeds confidence like success.

There are basically three places most salespeople consistently look for business—their own home, their own office, everywhere else. Unfortunately, many new salespeople only have the confidence or skills to feel comfortable looking for buyers in the first two places until they're too frustrated and burnt out even to think about prospecting "everywhere else."

Just as we in the sales industry will create incentives that "motivate" consumers to engage in the unpleasant act of parting with their money, you as well can utilize a series of incentives or rewards that will motivate *you* to keep your goal of regularly and consistently prospecting for buyers. You may only need an incentive program until the financial gains from your increased production becomes a sufficient enough reward as well as incentive to get it done—and done right.

The hungry cat makes the best hunter.

The first step to self-motivation is to be *prepared*. Before you get going, you must first *get ready*.

Preparation for most salespeople is the least understood and unfortunately least applied part of their careers—and it should be the most focused on. President Abraham Lincoln once said, "If given eight hours to chop down a tree—I would spend the first seven sharpening my axe." The best time to buy an umbrella is *before* it starts to rain.

If you have broken down your particular industry's hit ratio (contacts to sales ratio), then you already have a good idea of *what* you must do to achieve your production goals. The concept of self-motivation addresses the issue of *why* you must do those things. Most of us will do just about *anything* if we can find a good enough reason. And making more money than you ever dreamed possible is hopefully a *good enough reason*.

The best time to focus on the motivation (why) to prospect is just before and during your prospecting activities. The two times a professional boxer needs to motivate himself the most is during the fight itself and when he first steps into the ring. That means an entire career spanning years boils down to just a few important minutes—repeated over and over again. Every boxer knows their mental state of mind *before* going into the ring determines the results of their activities *in* the ring. After a while, the ability to self-motivate during crucial times becomes as natural a part of their career as training and fighting in the ring.

So how does a boxer self-motivate himself to engage in one of the most brutal sports of all time? He does not focus on the hours of grueling training or the punishment he must endure in the ring; he sees only the Title Belt around his waste at the end of it all. The boxer—just like the sales professional—understands that everything else is just a means to an end; and the end justifies the means.

The key is to focus on the pleasant "results" of the activity more than on the activity itself or the unpleasantness you may associate with it. Here's a little mental tip to help you stay positive, even after a negative experience prospecting. Let's say you get a negative response when calling prospects on the telephone; do not stand up and take a break after you hang up, even for a few seconds. To distract yourself momentarily from the negative experience will be your natural first instinct and even sounds like the best thing to do, especially after a particularly negative encounter. But it's not. For primarily psychological reasons, stay in your seat, pick up the phone, and make another call—and keep making calls until you get a positive response. End every round by delivering a punch, not receiving one. You never ever want your latest prospecting experience to be a negative one. It will make it all the much harder to restart again, even if it's only a few minutes later.

The Prospecting Track

1. **Verify:** Always make sure that any new prospect you encounter has the capacity or at least the authority to make the purchase. I can't even imagine how many realtors over the years gave full blown sales presentations to tenants.

2. **Introduce:** Don't overlook the method you use to introduce yourself to others. First impressions are crucial, and you never get a second chance to make them. Make your approach project confidence and likeability. In addition to your name, also include who you represent and your professional title (if any).

3. **Show concern:** You can quickly and easily show concern for someone during your greeting or introduction. We do it all the time—"How are you today?"

4. **Give reason/benefit:** State the reason you are approaching them and the benefits they will receive at least by hearing you out. Example: "I sell security systems (the reason) that literally pay for themselves through drastic reductions in your insurance premiums (the benefit).

5. **Ask:** Ask for the sale. It's that simple. In fact, statistically speaking, salespeople have to "ask" for the sale three times before the prospect says yes once.

6. **Ask another way:** If you get a "no" to your first request for the sale, shortly thereafter ask them for the sale using slightly different verbiage or using a slightly different approach. If you ask the second time for the sale exactly the same way you asked the first time, the pros-

pect may interpret that as you weren't listening to him the first time, or simply don't care he already said no. Different verbiage might include something like, "Now that I've given you some additional benefits of buying the product, are you sure you won't reconsider a purchase at this time?"

7. Ask for the referral: If you didn't get a "yes" to your first two requests for the sale, then you still have one more shot—just maybe with a different buyer. "I understand you're not interested at this time, but before I let you go, is there anyone else that you can think of that may benefit from or have a need for my product?" Then just like every other closing question, shut up until they give you an answer.

8. Thank you: This is always the last step regardless of how the previous steps turned out. Salespeople should use the words "thank you" more often than they use their own name.

I know one of the primary fears among any newer salesperson is the always dreaded question, "How long have you been selling _____?" Repeat after me, *"They're just curious!"* I mean it—they're just curious. Here's your standard answer: "Boy it seems like forever." At which point they'll probably chuckle, nod their head in agreement—and never bring it up again.

Your particular industry or sales organization may have already provided you with some form of prospecting scripts and dialogues. What I have listed below is a simple and effective formula for you to operate within using your individual style, dialogue, and industry guidelines.

1. **Introduce: This is usually a simple hello followed by your name and the organization's name you are representing. Here's a tip: Smile when you make your introduction. Believe it or not, your words will sound more upbeat and sincere, even over the telephone. Receptionists do this all the time. Smiling when you speak actually makes you sound more pleasant and likeable.**

2. **Qualify – concern: If you are calling a specific prospect, immediately following your introduction, you must "qualify" that the person you *want* to speak to is indeed the person you have on the line. You can ask if he is (name of the person you are calling for), or you can use a general qualifying question such as, "Are you the homeowner?" You can even simply ask them *their* name to initiate the dialogue.**

Also show concern for the intrusion—"Have I reached you at a bad time?"

3. **State your Business: Get out the cue cards if necessary. Read, tell, relate, convey, assert...*sing* if you're able, but state the reason for the call—quickly! Prospects are the most impatient with strangers the first few seconds of contact.**

The dialogue here is simple, "The reason I'm calling is…."

4. **Qualify: The question at this point is are they interested in continuing the conversation? You can ask them—and watch your hit ratio plummet. Or you can just assume they are interested and keep right on talking. If they ask you a buying question or indicate they're receptive to your call in some way, then keep going. So far, they're qualified.**

5. **Rapport: I have always found humor the quickest and most effective way to establish rapport. Once you have completed the above four steps, don't be afraid to interject a humorous remark or anecdote. If possible, try to reference something the prospect says during the initial stages of the conversation. For example, during the** *qualifying* **stage you may ask if the person you are speaking to is the homeowner. If he says yes, a humorous reference at that point might be, "Great. Then I'm speaking to the king (or queen) of the castle."**

6. **Close #1: Ask for the sale (directly) the first time.**

7. **Close #2: Ask for the sale again, using slightly different verbiage and/or approach.**

8. **Close #3: Ask for the referral.**

The key to any successful marketing campaign is numbers—and lots of them. Face-to-face contact is still the best way to get your message directly to consumers, but thanks to bulk mail systems and the Internet, you can now prospect millions of potential customers all over the world with just the click of a button. These mediums allow you to work *smarter* as opposed to *harder,* as well as prospect in numbers way beyond anything you could accomplish on an individual basis.

Here are two important factors to keep in mind when utilizing electronic or bulk mail content:

1. **The seven second rule. You have a mere seven seconds to convey to the recipient who you are, what you are selling, and where or how they can make a purchase. The bad news is that seven seconds includes the time it takes the prospect to open the envelope and/ or email. So make your message immediately obvious and memorable.**

2. **Regardless of the marketing** *method,* **the marketing** *message* **should always be the same—***BUY NOW!* **Remember, with indirect marketing there is no personal contact or opportunity to create rapport. If the prospect doesn't act or at least make a decision to purchase within thirty seconds upon receiving your message, he never will.**

I have engaged in just about every prospecting scenario (adventure) you can imagine. When dozens of phone calls failed, I've actually worn a disguise in order to get past a security guard at the front desk to gain access to the CEO upstairs. I have sold products door-to-door where the biggest fear of *failure* I had was my inability to outrun the guard dog to the gate.

(Author's Note: Before I forget, for all you door-to-door sales professionals out there, sooner or later you're probably going to have to make that mad dash back to the gate with old Fido on your heels. If you ever encounter an aggressive or charging dog, remember this bit of advice from a guy who's knocked thousands of doors over the years. Stop right where you are, do not turn and run (attacking dogs love that), stay calm, stand tall, and in an assertive voice say, "Wanna take a bath? C'mon, let's go…in the tub…c'mon, let's take a bath." I'd be shocked if that dog takes one more step. None of the one's I used it on ever did, except one—the filthiest dog I've ever seen. Thankfully, I beat him to the gate.)

Here's the bottom line to all sales prospecting. Stop thinking, acting, and talking like prospecting is a bad thing. Not only is it not a *bad* thing, it's the *only* thing that can make you rich in this business!

"I come up with the meaning of life and you call it torture?"

WILLIAMS (MOVIE: THE BEST OF TIMES)

CHAPTER 27: MARKETING VERSUS SELLING

"50% of all advertising works. The only problem is, we don't know which 50%." — LEE IACCOCA

I n this chapter, we'll discuss some basic marketing techniques and strategies that you can tailor to your individual selling situations. In many ways, the product or service you sell is secondary to *how* you sell it.

Thanks to the Internet and other electronic mediums, the whole world is now your market. There are no corners for anyone to corner anymore. An individual using a five-hundred-dollar PC now has access to the exact same sales resources as the world's largest corporations. Thanks to the new global market, we as salespeople now have an unlimited quantity of marketing venues and options. The market is too vast for any single entity to dominate any significant portion of it.

Amazon, hailed as the world's largest book seller, sells pretty much the exact same books most book sellers sell. It's not *what* Amazon sells that makes them so successful—it's *how* they sell it. The product or service you sell is almost secondary to how you sell it—effective marketing leads to successful selling.

Here are the basic principles of effective product marketing.

1. **Know thy product: Product knowledge creates product enthusiasm and product enthusiasm creates product sales. It's that simple. Learn enough about your product to get excited enough about it to want to share that excitement and enthusiasm with your market. If you can't get enthusiastic about the particular product you are currently selling, it may be time to start selling a product you can get excited about.**

2. **Know thy market and thy customer: Understand they are two different beasts. For instance, Amazon's "market" is anyone with access to the Internet. Their "customers" are those who purchase books over the Internet. All of Amazon's customers may be Internet users but not all Internet users are Amazon customers. Amazon knows their "market" appeal is** *how* **they sell—and their customer appeal is** *what* **they sell.**

3. **Above all, sell thyself: Again, using the Amazon example, Amazon doesn't sell books as much as it sells** *itself***. They no longer need to successfully sell their products to their customers because they have effectively sold themselves to their market. Their name alone tells their market who they are, what they sell, and where their products can be purchased. All of those things come with the territory when you have effectively sold** *yourself***.**

When I conduct my seminars on personal and product marketing, the first round of questions I get from the audience usually deals with the costs involved with creating an effective and profitable marketing campaign. When it comes to advertising, there's *cost*, there's *price*, and there's *value*. The "cost" is the monetary value of doing something versus not doing it. The "price" is the actual amount spent, and the "value" is the return you see from the expense of advertising. The question with any advertising efforts is if you will get your money's worth. Marketing isn't just *spending*; it's *investing*, which implies some kind of return on your investment. Spending without the certainty of a return is called gambling. "Investing" is depositing one dollar and withdrawing three.

All too many salespeople take the approach that they can't start spending money on advertising until they start making money from selling. Let's take that conclusion a bit further. Imagine yourself as a surgeon and your career as the patient.

How would you like to be your "career" lying on the operating table about to undergo surgery and the doctor (you) says, "I'm glad you decided to let me operate—now I'll have enough money to attend medical school...it's always been a dream of mine."

It takes money to make money. Actually, it takes *spending* some of that money to make money. Or in the case of marketing, spending it *before* you can make it.

Before the Internet, businesses would create a niche for their particular product or service, founded upon consumer *demand*, and then salespeople would rush in to exploit that niche, providing the *supply* directly to the consumer. The Internet took the established sales concept of supply and demand and added it to it convenience and variety as additional buying motivators. Up to half of the goods and services consumers purchase today are purchased simply because they are easy to locate and buy and offer a large variety of selections. As soon as we become aware of anything we'd like to buy (moment of truth), we can find out where to acquire it and literally have it purchased and on its way to us within minutes. Just the ability for consumers to do that is a market in and of itself.

What this means to you as an individual salesperson is that you can take any product or service, plug it into a global marketing network that 90 percent of the consumers worldwide have access to, and begin selling immediately, simply because it's *there*. It helps to have a product or service that is in demand among consumers, but today, just making it easy to find and purchase *helps* even more.

For salespeople, the Internet is a two-way street of opportunity. Consumers can use the net to come to you and you can use the net to go to them. The most common methods for *going to* the consumer are by email or advertising placements with web sites and search engines (banner ad and link exchange). Some methods cost money and others are accessible for free. They're all out there; you just have to locate which ones are best for you and your budget.

The Internet allows you the ability not only to access information and resources, but also to be a provider of information and resources to other net users and potential customers. This means that you are not only using your products and services to attract potential customers, but also using additional information and resources to attract them as well, in the hope that those seeking additional information will take the additional step of making a purchase while they're at it.

What you *offer* consumers must include a lot more than just what you *sell* them.

This is not a how-to manual for Internet marketing. I am simply providing the basics for you to then go out and do the necessary research on your own to enact some of the strategies we discuss here. All the information you need is out there, literally at your finger tips. I'll tell you what to look for.

Many of the systems and strategies I'll be discussing were gained from my direct experience in those areas. I am currently co-owner of a very successful Internet marketing firm, Evergreen Marketing, Inc. You can visit us on the web at EvergreenMarketingInc.com. We were pioneers in the field of Internet and e-database marketing. In the next two chapters, I will discuss in more detail database and Internet marketing. But for now, we'll discuss the three main pillars to a successful database marketing system.

When it comes to selling anything, whether on the Internet or not, anytime anyone shows any interest in what you're selling, that prospect is worth staying in touch with until he *buys or dies*—or refers you to someone else who will. That means you must create a system for attracting and managing those prospects who have exhibited at least some interest in you or your offering and have given you permission to contact them in the future with related information and opportunities. The most common method is signing up for certain web site's mailing list where they send you periodic emails (newsletters) relating to them and/or your particular topic of interest.

I am not talking about spam, which is *unsolicited* correspondence. That means the receiver did not give you direct permission to send them emails. Even if they willingly provided you their email address, that doesn't mean you have their expressed permission to contact them. Notice what I said in the above paragraph, "and have given you permission to contact them in the future." This type of database is called opt-in. Opt-in means they have given you written permission to send them your information at the email address they provided.

There are two types of opt-in lists. The first is called *exclusive*. Meaning only the entity you gave that address to will be sending you *their* information. The other type of list is called *shared* or *non-exclusive*. This is where the entity you provided your email address to then goes out and sells or rents your email address (along with your written permission) to other entities who will then, in turn, start sending you *their* material. That's why when you purchase a product over the Internet, such as flowers, before long you are receiving dozens of emails about flowers from web sites and companies you never heard of before.

How do you know which type of opt-in list you're signing up for? *Read the fine print* before hitting the "I Agree" button. Every opt-in database my companies offer all state clearly that we never share the respondents email address with any other person or entity. Which is why we have over 750,000 opt-in members worldwide and one of the best reputations in the business.

Database Mining: This is the compilation of email addresses of Internet users, ideally those who have expressed an interest in your topic and/or given you permission to contact them by email. Databases can be purchased or created from outside third parties who specialize in such activities, or created *in-house* by you and/or your organization. Email addresses can include past clients if they have given you permission to contact them in the future. That's why most e-commerce sites offer you the opportunity to opt-in to their newsletter to receive additional information and savings. All they are trying to do is compile their in-house database for future marketing efforts. You do not need the recipient's permission to send hard or snail-mail to any physical address. Opt-in restrictions do not apply.

Database Management: This is the actual "working" of the list. Any email and/or hard mail database must be properly managed. Especially Internet email lists since they fall under tighter regulations. For instance, every bulk email you send to your database must give the recipient the clear option of opting-out of your database and receiving no future mailings from you. Once an opt-in subscriber has requested they no longer be contacted by you, you must remove that recipient's email address from your database in a "timely manner." If you continue to send emails to anyone who has opted out of your database or anyone else who has requested you send them no future emails, you are now violating spam laws and will—not might, but "will"—have your web site shut down and your domain name black-listed, which means no hosting company will touch you with a ten foot pole. It's as if your web site is gone forever. And one disgruntled email recipient can do that to you.

(Author's Note: Please read and understand what I am about to share with you. A disgruntled re-

cipient can lodge a spam complaint against your web site and get it shut down, even if you never sent them a single email! You've probably seen those companies on the net that promise they can send your advertisement to millions of potential customers worldwide for a few hundred dollars. Well, they probably can send your advertisement to millions of people—just not people who opted-in to receive "your" advertisement. That's called spam. Even if the recipient opted-in to receive the bulk mailing company's emails, they didn't opt-in to receive yours. Also, different bulk email compa-nies have different definitions of "opt-in." To some, stealing email addresses from an online directory is close enough.)

Database Marketing: This is your actual (and le-gal) bulk hard mail and e-marketing campaigns using the databases you have compiled and/or have access to. I will discuss specific techniques in the next two chapters.

There is one concept I want you to keep in mind during all of your marketing planning and practic-es: *Positioning*. This signifies not only *who* you are but *where* you are in relation to your market and customer base. A key positioning ground for the In-ternet would be search engines and other online directories. Even a slight advantage in position-ing can dramatically increase your market share and sales—just like a slight deficiency in your posi-tioning can spell disaster. For example, when you conduct a keyword search on the net using any one of the numerous online search engines available, your search probably results in thousands of pages containing hundreds of thousands of web sites, web pages, and links related to the keywords you entered. Despite those millions of options, I'm willing to bet that 90 percent of the time, you find the resource you're searching for on the very *first* page that usually list the top dozen or so resources that match your inquiry. If so, you're just the like the rest of us. That is where "positioning" comes in. The difference between the resource/link at the very bottom of the *first* page and at the resource/link at the very top of the *second* page is basically one line of one page. But the difference in the number of click-thrus each entity receives is astronomical! Simply because 99 percent of users never make it to the second page—positioning!

There's also another type of positioning that takes place and this is in the minds and perceptions of your customers as to how they relate to and feel about your particular product, service, organization, or even industry. The key to positioning yourself and your offerings favorably in the market place of the consumers mind will depend upon successfully establishing the necessary awareness and rapport with your client base, as well as separating yourself and your product from the competition. An effective marketing plan can accomplish all of those things for you, and pretty quickly, given all the options at your disposal today that weren't even available a few short years ago. It's time to *take advantage of your advantage.*

These are the four components of marketing. You must understand these components and how they directly relate to the others in order to develop an effective marketing *plan of action*.

1. **Defensive: This component is comprised of tactics and programs designed to maintain or defend the current or existing market share.**

2. **Offensive: This component would include all proactive marketing efforts to gain** *new* **or additional market share and customers. Every effective marketing plan of action has an offensive component to continually gain market share and customers lost due to normal attrition. Even the big boys are always looking for ways to get bigger.**

3. **Strategy: This component consists of the planning, development and execution of your defensive and offensive marketing plans of action.**

4. **Positioning: This component is the culmination of the previous three components. Any deficiencies in the first three will surely have a negative impact on your ability to position yourself effectively. Get the first three right and this one's a given. The position you are obviously trying to attain and hold is the** *number one* **position in your respective market—or at least in the minds of your consumers. And remember, in the mind of your consumers there is no reality—only perceived reality.**

When conveying the message that will create the desired impression in the consumers mind, remember always to reinforce the following:

1. **Who you are**

2. **What you sell**

3. **Where you can be contacted or your offerings purchased**

The first step in planning your marketing strategy is to set effective yet *realistic* goals. This includes creating an advertising budget sufficient to achieve your "realistic" objectives. Next, you will need to develop your marketing plan of action. That means identifying who you will be targeting, what your message will be, and all the methods you can utilize to deliver that message. Then you will need to start identifying, acquiring, and utilizing the proper tools to get the job done. And not just done—*but done right.*

Whatever marketing tools and materials you use in the selling and promotion of yourself and your product, you should always convey to the consumer or receiver of your message an image of quality, trust, and competence, ideally, in a likeable and memorable manner. The best way to stay "memorable" is to keep your marketing efforts, tools, and materials what I call *consistently persistent.* In other words, find what works and stick with it until it stops working or you find something else that works better.

Consumers don't buy products as much as they buy *trust.* Again using Amazon as an example, there are countless venues for consumers to purchase books from online. But who do consumers *trust* most with their credit card and billing information? I'll give you a hint...it's also the same venue they purchase the most books from. Remember, again, what I said earlier about offering more than just what you sell? Amazon not only sells books to its customers; it throws in peace of mind—a bargain at any price!

Many companies employ very sophisticated marketing strategies that actually identify and utilize specific key or hot-button words that act as language triggers designed to increase awareness about or direct attention toward a specific product or entity. Just the terminology used in some advertisements actually increases a consumer's desire or emotions toward a particular product or service.

Here is a list of what a recent national study determined were the twelve most persuasive words in advertising.

1. **Discover**

2. **Easy**

3. **Health**

4. **Love**

5. **Money**

6. **New**

7. **Proven**

8. **Results**

9. **Safety**

10. **Save**

11. **Guaranteed**

12. **You**

Did you catch that last one? One of the most effective marketing strategies a salesperson can use is to make the prospect feel special or unique. That's why one of the cardinal rules of selling is to use the customer's name—and use it often.

Rather than trying to go out there and re-invent the wheel, so to speak, it may behoove you to turn certain aspects of your marketing campaign over to the professionals. There are plenty of effective and reputable organizations out there that specialize in bulk and Internet marketing campaigns. Find a good one, and if the price and results are right, use them.

Next to face-to-face selling, Internet and direct mail selling are the most effective mediums to get your message out and bring customers in. The primary benefit of mass marketing campaigns is their convenience, cost, and efficiency. They allow you to prospect more customers faster and for less expense. What bulk marketing campaigns lack in *quality* they are designed to make up for in *quantity*. Which leads us back to the basic premise of all selling; *it's a numbers game*.

One advantage mass marketing systems offer in addition to their ability to reach large numbers of prospects *where they live*, is the added efficiency of being able to delegate minor tasks to reliable third parties, saving you time and money while allowing you to pursue higher priority tasks. You can't make a million dollars doing five-dollar-an-hour stuff, but you can make a million dollars paying someone else five dollars an hour to help you find customers—working *smarter* not just *harder*.

Here are some common *dos and don'ts* when it comes to mass marketing campaigns.

DOs:

1. **Set minimum activity goals. Mass marketing must be done on a massive and consistent scale in order to be fully effective. Doing 10 percent less in your mass marketing campaigns may cost you a reduction in sales of 25 percent or more. Mass marketing, unlike other methods of prospecting, has a cumulative and exponential success rate. You need to identify that "minimum" number of contacts you must send to, and how regularly you must send to them in order to achieve the production goals you have set for the program. This will take some experimenting on your part until you can create**

the right message and delivery venue that works best for you.

2. Be consistent. Mass marketing programs are one of the few advertising mediums where it's okay to bombard the recipients with the same (or very similar) message over and over again. The key is consistent repetition. Find a look and style that yields the best results for you, then stick with it—forever. Consistency is the key to positioning.

3. Be persistent. Or better yet, be *consistently persistent.* Also remember what I said above about mass marketing mediums requiring minimum contact numbers on a consistent and regular basis in order for the campaign to catch its stride, so to speak, before it can begin achieving its maximum results. For instance, if you send the same message to the same group of recipients five times in a row, that same group will yield greater results with every subsequent mailing—the fifth contact yielding the most. You must be persistent enough to stick with your system until it begins to produce its cumulative and exponentially increasing results. Success often means hanging on after everyone else has let go.

4. Use quality materials. I can't stress this enough, especially when it comes to direct mail items. I personally never read any piece of junk mail that actually looks like "junk." Spend the extra 2¢ a copy.

5. Update your mailing lists often. Remember what I said earlier about "managing" your databases. Database management includes regular *house-cleaning* to re-

move unwanted contacts from the lists (which in some cases is required by law). There is also the normal attrition rate of mined and purchased lists. People move and change their email addresses regularly. Any mass mail list, even just a few months old, is well on its way to becoming obsolete. Since you will probably be using third party mailing entities to send on your behalf, you will need a system to insure that your messages are indeed being delivered to every recipient and in an acceptable manner. The best way to do this is by *seeding* the list of your sender. That means you request that your mail sending entity include you in their database as a recipient for every mailing they do for you. If there is a problem with *your* mailing, then it's safe to say that others on the list are having a similar problem. Any reputable mailing entity will be able to provide you tracking and receiving statistics from each mailing. You seed the list to confirm those statistics.

6. Use the clients name whenever possible. Who is this "occupant" person anyway, and why does he keep sending his junk mail to my house? But don't worry; to ensure his privacy, *I never read any of it*.

7. Market you and your product as opposed to just "selling" you and your product. There is a difference and, hopefully, this book has helped demonstrate that.

DON'Ts:

1. Never use language, images, or materials that a nun or a five-year-old would find offensive. You risk almost certain alienation of the recipient.

2. Avoid, when possible, general salutations such as "oc-cupant" and "resident" or other impersonal terms.

3. Never use middle names or middle initials. Ego thing I guess?

4. Try to use Mr., Mrs., Ms., or Miss when possible if the first name or initial is unknown.

5. Don't forget the *Seven Second Rule*. The average amount of time the average consumer is exposed to any mass marketing medium is seven seconds.

"Coming together is a beginning; Keeping together is progress; Working together is success."

HENRY FORD

CHAPTER 28: PERSONAL POWER MARKETING

"It ain't braggin' if you can back it up." Jay "Dizzy" Dean (four time twenty-game winner and member of MLB's Hall of Fame)

A sk the average salesperson what he sells, and he will usually reply with the particular product or service he is offering. Ask the average sales "professional" what he sells and you'll get the *truth: Himself!*

What's in a name? There is a particular hamburger restaurant in my native Southern California that sells the best tasting hamburgers I've ever eaten. I know this as a direct result of years of extensive research on the subject. Directly across the street from that establishment is a nationally known franchise that also specializes in selling hamburgers. The prices are pretty much comparable at both locations. What is not comparable is the amount of business done by the two establishments.

The national chain with their *inferior* offering probably outsells the better tasting and equally priced hamburger just across the street, ten to one. Why? Because consumers will often select one brand over another based less on "what" they are buying and more on "who" is doing the selling. This means your name and the image it represents are more important than the actual goods and services you happen to be selling.

Those nationally recognized hamburger chains spend millions of dollars every year getting the consumers to buy *them* before those consumers even get hungry for a burger, which means the sale is made before the order is even placed.

When I say "personal" marketing, I mean using the exact same techniques and strategies the big corporations have been using on us most of our lives, but only on a smaller more individual scale.

What the large corporations are really trying to sell is *us*. Selling *us* on at least the perception *they* are superior (not just their products or services) to the competition. Advertisers try to create that superior perception in one of two ways—by demonstrating specifically that their product or service is superior and/or anything else offered by a competitor is inferior.

 "The best way to knock the competition is to *never* knock the competition." Unless you can do it in a way that doesn't seem like you're knocking them.

Whether it be building you up or taking your competitors down a notch, the key here is good taste and common sense. If there are aspects to a competitor's products or services that are inferior to yours, then by all means you must inform the consumer about those deficiencies. Unless there is major selling point that needs to be explained in greater detail, the best approach is to demonstrate why your offering is superior as opposed to how a competitor's is inferior. There are tactful ways to demonstrate that you are superior without saying someone else is inferior.

When a potential client would ask me how my particular sales organization stacked up against the others, I would say, "Let me answer that question this way; if there was a company out there that offered a better product or service, I'd be working *there*…but I'm not." Then I'd leave it at that. I knocked the competition without even mentioning their names.

The objectives of an effective personal marketing campaign are to separate you from your competition in a meaningful and memorable way, and create an image and perception of likeability and trust toward you, your organization, as well as your particular product or service. If done effectively, you will have already sold your consumers on you and what you're selling before it ever comes time for them to make the purchase. Your entire campaign is designed to establish some kind of commitment from your market that, when it comes time to buy, they buy from you.

The best case scenario would be to initiate your campaign in a way that hopefully provides some kind of initial success. An early payday, so to speak, is the best way for you to establish a long term commitment to the program. You know how we are as salespeople; if something doesn't work right away it's time to move on. But your personal marketing campaign is a career long endeavor. Once you establish the initial image you are trying to create, then all marketing efforts from that point on will be coordinated and consistent with your initial program.

Consistency in advertising creates awareness and awareness creates recognition. This means using *consistent* designs, logos, slogans, colors, materials, and so on. Basic rule of thumb: Anything with your name on it should look exactly like everything else with your name on it. If you walk in to any one of those nationally known hamburger chains and pick up *anything*—a menu, placemat, food wrapper, *whatever*—I'll bet within two seconds you'll know exactly which burger franchise you are in and probably most of what's on their menu without ever seeing or hearing their name. Just by their color scheme and logo, consumers know who they are and what they sell. The question is, how did those national franchises determine which colors, slogans, and so on, are the most effective in creating an image of likeability and trust in the minds of their consumers? The same way you're going to—only for millions of dollars less.

Remember, not only are you a *provider* of goods and services, you are also a *consumer* of them as well, a consumer swayed by the same emotional and marketing influences as everyone else. The same selling techniques that have been working "on" you should be just as effective working "for" you if properly applied. For lack of a better term, you'll be acting as your own lab rat.

Example one: Years ago I owned a car that was so dilapidated and downright ugly, I was not only embarrassed to be seen driving it, I was also embarrassed to even have it parked in my driveway. Needless to say, I only drove it around town when I absolutely had to. On the other hand, if my car at the time had been a brand new Rolls Royce, I would have probably *lived* in it, not to mention put a few thousand miles on it every week.

Example two: I once spent twenty-five dollars on a box of standard business cards. Unfortunately, they arrived two days after my business phone number was changed. No problem, I simply took a pen and crossed out the old number and wrote the new number next to it. It took me the next several months to distribute those one hundred cards. Sometime later, I spent one hundred dollars on a box of the most awesome business cards I've ever seen. I actually framed one! It took me less than two weeks to hand them all out.

Moral of the story: If your marketing tools look like my old car then they'll spend more time in the driveway than on the road. From now on, view every item of marketing material as you would the vehicle you drive.

I have a friend who tried to save a few bucks by brewing his own beer. I even tasted it once. My first reaction was, "Where do I spit this?" which is probably the same reaction my prospects had when I handed them a business card with my phone number written in pen. Their second thought was probably relief that it wasn't scribbled in crayon.

Spend the extra few dollars, or whatever it takes to make sure you have the most memorable and impressive marketing materials of anyone in your office, if not your market, if not your industry. It is the absolute best investment you can make. Believe me, if you are not happy with your marketing materials and message you will probably lack the necessary enthusiasm to deliver them to the buying public effectively. Professional selling basically requires confidence and promotion. Effective personal marketing increases your confidence to increase your promotion.

In order for your marketing materials to look professional, they should probably be designed and created by a "professional," which does not include your office's copy machine. Many marketing materials can be designed and purchased directly online or from a local retailer.

The theme behind developing a personal marketing campaign and materials is to make them exactly that—personal. The central theme of all your marketing materials and efforts should be "you." Remember, that's what you *really* sell. Here are some keys to keep in mind when planning and developing your "Personal Identity Kit."

1. 1. The key word is "personal." Don't be afraid to show a more casual or personal side of yourself. I have seen many printed materials and online sources depicting non-business content or images while still maintaining a professional context. I once knew a salesperson who used a photograph of himself fishing on his boat as his primary business photo. It was literally on all of his materials. Even though there was an emphasis on a non-business side of him, he was still very professional and very successful. Not only was the image he presented a casual and likeable one, it was also *memorable*—proven by the fact I am mentioning that salesperson now and I haven't seen him or his marketing materials in over twenty years.

I stopped being shocked by the image some salespeople present in their marketing efforts and materials. I've seen professional business photos of salespeople that contained cats, dogs, birds, and even a giant lizard of some kind—wearing a miniature cowboy hat! I've seen photos of salespeople wearing everything from a tuxedo to a tank top and shorts while running in a marathon. One salesperson in my adopted state of Maine even depicts himself wearing full hunting regalia. Although these personal themes may vary slightly, they all have the same common goal; to instill in their consumers an image and perception of likeability and trust that says to the consumer, *this person is just like me*—especially if I happen to own a giant lizard with a thing for western apparel.

Personal marketing and professional marketing come together to create an image for consumers that shows them you are also a *person* and not just a *salesperson*. It's a lot easier to say "no" to a salesperson than it is to just a person—especially a person just like you.

2. **All of your materials should ideally get and maintain the attention and interest of the viewer. And as we discussed earlier, you have about seven seconds to accomplish this. Your materials should say, "Pick me up; read me; I'm important." Bright colors, attractive schemes, and catchy slogans all help create that message, when combined with a unique and creative method of delivering them. Take the next week or so to make note of any form of advertising you encounter that immediately grabs your attention or interest, particularly specific aspects of the medium that had the biggest impact on you. Chances are if it worked for them on you, then it may work for you on them.**

I even recommend compiling your own advertising reference guide. It can be as simple as a notebook that lists and keeps track of any exceptional forms of advertising and marketing you encounter as well any specific aspects that attracted your attention or interest.

The key is to find advertising mediums and venues that you yourself appreciate, then modify them to your particular image, market, product, and so on. One of the best ways to create, enhance, and customize other advertiser's marketing ideas and approaches is to use a compilation of the best aspects each advertiser offers. In other words, take the best of what everyone else is doing and combine them to make your own *greatest hits*.

3. **Try to make your materials memorable and retainable whenever possible. This means attaching to your message an important and noteworthy feature that hopefully will motivate the recipient to retain the feature, along with your message (sales pitch), well beyond the initial seven second contact. The best way to make sure the prospect retains your message is to make sure he retains the "messenger."**

A common method for accomplishing retention among consumers is to physically attach your sales message to a retainable item, such as your business information printed on a calendar you then distribute to your client base. They retain your business information for an entire year hanging right there on their wall. I'll bet you right now, from where you're sitting, you can see at least a half dozen items that are currently advertising a product or service. Is there a company name printed on your pen? A coffee mug with your favorite sports team logo? Anything you might even be wearing? Is there someone's magnetic business card on any of the appliances in your home? Why do you think restaurants have to-go menus?

Here's another common *keeper* we all deal with—coupons. All of those items are specifically designed to be nothing more than an advertisement the recipient has a reason to hang on to or act upon in the case of coupons or special offers. In some cases, we may actually pay money to receive certain advertisements—subscription TV commercials for instance, or the twenty five dollar New England Patriots mug sitting on my desk right now.

Ineffective advertising costs money. Effective advertising *pays for itself*.

Back when I sold real estate, the most common method of retainable advertising agents used, especially in their regular prospecting areas, were calendars with their name, photo, and contact information printed at the top. Every March 1, the local Boy Scout troop would stop by the office to pick up several cases of undelivered calendars (still packed neatly in their boxes), for their annual paper drive. And I need to add that it wasn't because the calendar printing company didn't get them delivered to those agents until February. They arrived every year at the same time—the last week of November of the previous year, plenty of time for a *motivated* agent to have them all distributed by January 1. When I would help the Boy Scouts load the cases of calendars into their van, I would always make note of the agent's names on the boxes of those calendars. It was like a crystal ball into their futures. I could tell by the name on the boxes which agents wouldn't be around next year to order new calendars.

4. Any marketing item that contains any information about you must have a look of quality and professionalism. Think of your marketing materials as your very own employees you've hired to work for you. You can hire professionals to do that work or you can hire amateurs. Again, stay away from the office copy machine.

5. Make it interesting and memorable by making it *different*. I have sent thousands of holiday cards over the years to prospects and clients that were appreciated and well received. But the one "holiday" card I always got the biggest and most positive response from was my annual "Happy Groundhog Day!" cards. Unique experiences tend to stand out and stay with us. How many times in your life have you ever received a Groundhog Day card? I rest my case.

6. Remember, selling is based more on "emotion" than it is on "logic." That's why I suggest using a more *human* or personal approach when developing "personal" marketing materials. People tend to get more emotional over personal issues as opposed to strictly business ones. The key here is to use a business approach, utilizing a personal aspect, to grab the recipient's attention in a way that relates back to the business aspect of your contact.

For example, a salesperson sending a holiday card to a prospect or client is a "business approach." Making it a *Groundhog Day* card utilizes a personal touch (humor) to quickly grab the recipients attention, that is then redirected to my sales and business information contained inside the card. My business approach was wrapped in my personal approach. Consumers receive dozens of *business* holiday cards every year. But all these years later, I'm still remembered by those clients as the only person on the planet who ever sent them a Groundhog Day card.

7. *Telling isn't selling.* **Telling is logic—selling is emotion. Telling is listing facts—selling is explaining benefits. Telling is a** *canned* **presentation—selling is a** *planned* **presentation. Telling is talking** *to* **a prospect—selling is talking** *with* **him.**

8. **Every marketing medium you use should immediately identify and reinforce who you are, what you sell, and where/how a prospect can find/buy what you're selling. If "you" are the primary source consumers have for locating and purchasing your product or service, then "you" and your contact information must be the** *primary* **message your materials convey. What good is pre-selling the client on "you" when that's the one thing he can't find when he needs to?**

Selling *who*, also means selling *where* and *how*— *where* you are and *how* you can be found. Thanks to the Internet, web site and email addresses are more valuable to salespeople these days than name and face recognition. Besides, you can't look up a *face* in the yellow pages or on Google.

9. **Keep all of your personal marketing efforts** *persistent and consistent* **just like we talked about in the last chapter. Any deviation from the consistency in your message may negate or limit your previous as well as future marketing efforts. It took Coke ninety-nine years to change their recipe! Find what works then stick with it.**

Some salespeople, especially those working for larger or franchise sales organizations, may have pre-established marketing guidelines their organization probably spent years and a small fortune developing. If this is the case and your governing organization's marketing restrictions do not allow you total control or creativity when it comes to every part of your personal marketing campaign, I'll bet there are still very effective "personal" marketing options already established within your organizational structure that you can *spice up* and make your own.

In some cases, the company may even provide some marketing materials for free where you only need to pay for your individual customization of the product.

If there is a corporate or institutional image already established for advertising by your organization, I recommend prior management or supervisor approval before spending any time or money in developing your own personalized marketing materials or program. There may even be copyright and/or standard practice policies regarding your particular organization's images and slogans where restrictions might apply in the usage of such materials even by employees of the organization. Better to ask permission first than to ask forgiveness later.

I used to conduct several seminars a year on personal and corporate marketing to the business and sales community. One of the most popular topics at those seminars was the development of what I call a *"Slogo."* That is a combination "logo" and "slogan," hence the name, "Slogo."

Creating an effective and memorable *Slogo* involves combining an image with a word, or displaying the image so that it appears as a word or phrase.

Here are a few examples of combining a logo with a slogan. One client my company developed a *Slogo* for was a salesperson with the last name of Bagwell. We took an image of a standard brown paper grocery bag and placed Bagwell's name inside of the image along with the phrase, *"It's in the bag with Bagwell."*

Another client we developed a program for happen to have the last name Coke. This one was easy. We designed a bottle cap with similar markings of a nationally known soft drink company (guess which one) and the slogan, *"Vince Coke... The real thing."*

The best place to start working on what your particular identity and image will look like is to pay a visit to some local retailers. I want you to casually (just like an average shopper would), but carefully, browse the aisles and see what jumps out at you or grabs your attention. Since certain colors or images attract your attention as a consumer, it stands to reason that some of those colors and images will also grab the attention of *your* consumers as well—no need to reinvent the wheel every time. Sometimes stealing a few of the neighbors hubcaps will do.

Select colors, images, and phrases that quickly get your attention or are attractive and appealing to you as a consumer. This will give you some useful tips when developing your final marketing program. Remember, those companies probably spent a considerable amount of time, effort, and money determining which colors and images were the most effective on consumers—time to play follow the leaders.

Remember what I said earlier about your personal marketing materials being more like your employees, out there working on your behalf? Let me spend ten minutes talking to the most junior employee of any organization and I will learn everything I need to know about that organization. In that case, the best the organization can hope for is that their employee conveys an image of quality and trust on behalf of the organization. The organization has two ways of accomplishing that goal. It can stand there beside the employee twenty-four-seven, and monitor everything the employee says and does. Or it can hire employees in the first place that are effective at conveying an image of quality and trust, even when the organization isn't there to make sure.

"All my life I wanted to be somebody. I see now I should have been more specific."

JANE WAGNER

CHAPTER 29: THE ART OF FOL-LOW-UP AND NETWORKING

"You don't come out a winner just by getting that first big order. The mark of a true pro is getting the re-order."

HARVEY MACKAY

Repeat after me, "No one will ever call me back!" In fact, say it again. "No one will ever call me back!"

This must be the attitude and belief of every salesperson who deals directly with the buying public. That means you either have to make the sale right then and there, or have an effective program of following up and networking with every client and every *potential* client you encounter, until they die or buy—or refer you to someone who will. Of course, the ideal situation for you as a salesperson is to have a marketing plan that effectively deals with both scenarios. Prospecting for clients without utilizing a system of follow up is like training a flock of homing pigeons then moving away.

Most salespeople already understand the importance of staying in touch with prospects who indicate an interest to purchase some time in the future, if not right then. But unfortunately, that's as far as most salespeople take it. They follow up with prospects almost as an activity as opposed to a specific plan of action or system.

I believe that the lack of a client/prospect follow-up system is the biggest characteristic of failure a salesperson can exhibit. Am I suggesting that the success of a salesperson depends on that little book full of names and numbers or that stack of business cards he keeps? That is *exactly* what I am suggesting!

Remember what I have been emphasizing to you all along—selling is more of a mental game than a physical one for the salesperson. Attitude, confidence, and enthusiasm are all *mental* states.

Now let me ask you this: What type of attitude, confidence, and enthusiasm is a salesperson exhibiting toward his long-term success in this business if he doesn't engage in activities here in the present to create business for himself in the future? That salesperson is exhibiting an attitude that reinforces to himself, *why bother following up with clients that won't buy for a year or so? It's not like I'll still be in the business then.* He is telling his mental state by his physical actions (or lack thereof) that he does not believe or see himself achieving long-term success in his career or current position.

"Whether we think we can or think we cannot... either way we are right" (Henry Ford).

That list of prospects you maintain contact with reinforces your belief that you are in this business for the long haul, and to confirm that fact, you must prospect *today* in order to gain business in the future. Therefore, you will need sales tomorrow as much as you need them today. By not maintaining a working follow-up system, you are sending a message to yourself, and that message is loud and clear: "Why bother following up or networking with these people? I won't be around when they need me anyway."

Hopefully, you now understand the importance of creating and maintaining an effective system of follow up for both your mental and financial well being.

As a real estate sales manager, I noticed that about 90 percent of the first listings or sales that newly licensed agents would get would result from a friend, family member, or referral from some other personal contact. In fact, many of the first few transactions many new agents were involved in dealt with somebody they knew in one capacity or another. I always felt the best way for newer salespeople to get their feet wet was to start in familiar territory where they were the most comfortable at felt most at home. In their own back yard, so to speak.

I recommend strongly that you establish a separate follow-up system for those prospects you have contact with on a personal basis such as friends, family, and your general sphere of influence. You never know where your next sale is going to come from. When it comes to being a salesperson, it's better to have a million friends than a million dollars.

The next concept may, at first, seem completely contrary to what we've been discussing so far regarding following up with potential prospects until they *buy or die.*

Don't chase—*replace.* You can only effectively network and follow up with so many prospects at any given time. Even with systems that allow you to manage huge databases electronically, you will still need to cull the herd, so to speak, periodically. There will still need to be a *quality* aspect to the *quantity* of prospects you follow up with in order to maximize the effectiveness of your system. You need to update your list on a regular basis and periodically get rid of the *dead wood,* and at the same time *replace* those lost contacts with new valid ones. This will enable you to direct more resources and time where they can be the most effective—with leads that offer a higher probability of a sale.

There are three primary factors that will determine the size of your follow-up database:

1. **Sales goals**

2. **Budget**

3. **How much prospecting you engage in now, to gain leads for the future**

A good place to begin establishing your networking and follow-up system is your existing or past client base. Remember, selling does not end with the sale. In fact, thanks to your effective follow-up system, the "sale" is just the beginning. I bet if you asked some of the top producers in your office, they will tell you that a sizable portion, if not the majority of their sales, come from repeat or referral business.

What is a referral? It is when someone you have had contact with has enough confidence in you and your offering to recommend someone he knows to you for business.

The best way to accomplish this is to constantly reinforce those who you expect to refer business to you by making sure they know:

1. **Who you are**

2. **What you sell**

3. **Where you or your offering can be found when needed**

Many times as a real estate agent, I would visit family and friends in my market place only to discover one of my competitor's "For Sale" signs in the front yard of my family member's neighbor, and often "good friend."

I would always ask them two questions—"Did you know your neighbor was thinking of selling before they listed with another agent?" and "Why didn't you tell them you had a friend or relative that was a realtor in this area when they first mentioned they were moving?" Their answer was always the same, "Oh, that's right! You sell real estate. It didn't even occur to us to tell them about you." Or just as worse, "Did you want us to let you know when we come across someone thinking about selling?" Now whose fault do you think that was? I was a secret agent! And I had no right to blame anyone else but myself for failing to blow my own cover.

A good way to get a steady flow of repeat and referral business is to *ask* for it. A better way to get a steady flow of repeat and referral business is to *keep asking* for it!

There is a common term used for follow-up systems. It's called "the pipeline." What's "in the pipe," so to speak, are the list of prospects you have put into your follow-up system (the pipe) that have yet to exit the other end as an actual sale. The more you prospect, the more future potential clients you have to put into your pipeline. The more prospects you put into your pipeline, the more that will come out the other end as sales. Your job is simple; keep stuffing *potential* clients into the pipe until it fills up enough to start pouring out *actual* clients from the other end. This will take the rest of your career—if you do it right.

The three primary objectives of any marketing plan that utilizes an effective follow-up system are:

1. **Make the sale**

2. **Get the re-sale**

3. **Find a reason to stay in touch or call them back (since they will never call you back)**

Remember, selling does not end with the sale. The problem is that most of your clients and prospects probably don't know that. That's where you come in and the teacher in you comes out. *You* must educate your prospects on your need and desire for future and referral business. Do not take it for granted that they will remember who you are and what you sell the next time they or someone they know has a need for it. Here are some keys to help with that.

1. **Ask—ask again—and keep asking. You must** *tell* **the prospect as often as possible that you want, need, appreciate, and deserve his repeat and referral business. You notice I said "deserve" his business. In other words, in some way you have earned the time and effort on his part to help provide you future business.**

How do you "earn" or "deserve" someone's referral and/or repeat business? Has anyone ever expressed a need to you for a certain product or service and you knew exactly who provided it, but said nothing? Why? Probably because you knew in your heart the person who provided that product or service didn't deserve the recommendation, or earn your confidence enough to make that recommendation.

2. This relates directly to number one above. Make sure the prospect understands that you respect and value your relationship with him and will do the same with anyone he recommends or refers to you. Many friendships have been lost over a business referral.

3. Be specific. Let the prospect know exactly what types of referral contacts you are interested in and how he can help identify and put them in contact with you.

4. When compiling the prospect list for your "pipeline," be sure to include as much information about the prospect as possible. This means personal as well as professional information. I'm not talking about corporate espionage or anything, but you'd be surprised at the positive response I would receive following up with a client when I asked about a sick friend or family member or even about his pet. Always include pet names. After a while, you'll understand why.

5. When approaching a prospect that has been referred to you by someone else, be sure to use the referring person's name as well as the positive and related aspects you share with him. Your message must be, the new client can trust you, since someone he trusts already trusts you. You don't actually have to say that, but try to imply it. Then of course live up to that trust.

6. Always utilize bulk or electronic mediums to save time and money; but whenever possible, do your networking and follow up directly with the prospect. Impersonal or bulk contacts are sort of like rodeo clowns; they serve a useful purpose, but they are still there to keep the bull

away from the rider—in this case, you away from the client.

7. Always identify a reason to follow up with a prospect. This could be a birthday, anniversary, or other meaningful event. It could be items you come across that may be of a personal or special interest to a particular prospect. I will often send an email, articles, or other information I come across that I feel a certain prospect might find interesting. How do I know what topics my clients might find interesting? I ask them. Then I retain that information in my follow-up system. Sometimes it's just a note to remind them I'm still in business and still need and want theirs. I always try to make contact if congratulation's for something the prospect has done or achieved is in order. Either way, never pass up an opportunity to follow up.

8. Follow up doesn't always mean long term. Whenever you get hit with the old, "Make it quick, I'm in a hurry," or, "I don't have time right now," or if there is in fact not sufficient time for your full sales presentation, never be afraid to reschedule. Let them know the information and/or opportunity you're calling to share with them is too important to hurry through. They will appreciate your professionalism and concern.

9. Mentally and physically prepare yourself for a follow-up contact as you would for any other *selling* situation. Remember, this is a professional call or contact disguised as a personal or friendly one. And they probably know it.

10. Remember that *how* and *why* you do your follow up and networking contacts are just as important as *when* you

do them. I have found that there are certain times when I am at my most effective mentally as a salesperson. Usually these high points come right after a sale or successful contact has been made. When I find myself *on a roll* so to speak, I try never to waste that enthusiasm and confidence after a positive experience by just doing business as usual, taking a break, or going back to the office. I reach out and share that confidence and enthusiasm with as many prospects as I can. I did what I recommend you do; take advantage of your advantage.

There are certainly numerous reasons to follow up with your prospects, but not one excuse not to. Here are six effective opportunities for following up or contacting prospects.

1. *"Look what I did."* **Whenever you do something of interest, don't be afraid to toot your own horn. Most people are happy to hear when someone they know has achieved something significant. I always let my client base know when I received an award or recognition for a professional accomplishment. That way, when they needed the services of a realtor, they hopefully chose one who seemed to know what he was doing and was good enough at it to get recognized for it.**

2. *"Look what you did."* **I never hesitated to contact someone, even if I had never contacted him before, to offer my congratulations or admiration for something he did. Yes, even my competitors.**

3. *"Who do you know?"* **Remember, you are looking for not only repeat but *referral* business as well. Let them know it and let them know it often.**

4. "*This is for you.*" **Over the years, I have probably sent a ton of notes, coupons, calendars, and the like to my clients. Most of it well appreciated, I'm sure, because I was always careful to choose promotional items I felt they would also retain, use, and appreciate.**

5. "*Don't forget me.*" **This would include any contact, direct or otherwise, that simply reminds the prospect you haven't forgotten about him—and to make sure he hasn't forgotten about you.**

6. "*If not now, then when*?" **If the prospect indicates he is not ready, willing, or able to make the purchase today, when does** *he* **think he** *will* **be ready? Go ahead and ask. You must record this information, even though it will probably change, then close the gap between now and then with an effective follow-up system—until he buys or dies. Rule of thumb: whatever time frame he gives you regarding when in the future he will be ready to buy—cut it in half.**

The old saying, "It's not *what* you know, it's *who* you know," applies more to selling than I think any other profession. The lack of follow up will cost you more money than all the sales you make combined. The money lost will far exceed the money gained. This is a statistical fact, since you will come across at least twice as many prospects who will buy but "just not right now" than you will prospects who will make the purchase right then and there.

The bottom line is this; working *with* your clients will make you far more successful than simply working *for* them.

"Snowflakes are one of nature's most fragile things, but look what they can do when they stick together."

The End

Do you know what it means when a dog is *ball crazy*? If you've ever seen or owned a dog that was "ball crazy," you know exactly what I mean. If not, let me explain. A good friend of mine trains service canines. He then provides them to various agencies, organizations, and individuals who employ the dogs for their specific purpose.

I once asked him how he knew which dogs would make the best service dogs. He explained that most of the service dogs he had trained over the years were rescued from local animal shelters and, contrary to popular belief, most of them were not puppies or specific breeds bred for certain purposes. I was obviously impressed with his ability to *teach old dogs new tricks*, so to speak. He then shared with me his secret. "You must find a dog that's *ball crazy*. Then you can teach them *anything* in a matter of days."

He explained that certain dogs, for whatever reason, were simply *ball crazy*. In other words, they were "crazy" for their ball or some other object of fascination, and would literally do *anything* to have access to the object of their desire. Their *primary* desire I might add.

He would walk down the aisles of the local animal shelter in front of the kennels bouncing a ball on the ground. He would then see which dogs went "crazy." If they met the age and physical requirements, he adopted them and began their training process.

"That's it?" I asked. "That's it," he replied. "Give me a dog that is ball crazy and I'll teach it anything in a matter of days." You see, a dog that is ball crazy is motivated in a way that other dogs are not. When a dog is ball crazy, that dog will choose his or her ball, or whatever the object is, over *everything* else—even food and water. When the dog responds positively to their training exercises, they would get to play with the ball as a reward. Just the sight of the ball would instantly gain the attention and obedience of the dog.

What is the current object of your desire? What ball drives you crazy? What motivates you more than anything else? What will you never fail to respond to? Everybody has a ball they're crazy about. What's yours?

Do you know what I looked for when hiring sales-people for the many organizations I worked for over the years? Those who were *ball crazy* for something. All I had to do then was identify what it was, then link the attainment of that object to a successful career in sales. Once they realized the fastest way of reaching their goals and obtaining their desires was to SELL LIKE CRAZY, they usually did.

Good hunting!

"The credit belongs to those people who are actually in the arena...who know the great enthusiasms, the great devotions to a worthy cause; who at best, know the triumph of high achievement; and who at worst, fail while daring greatly...so that their place shall never be with those cold and timid souls who know neither victory nor defeat"

PRESIDENT THEODORE ROOSEVELT

CPSIA information can be obtained at www.ICGtesting.com
Printed in the USA
LVIW010919291019
635574LV00006BA/89

9 781451 519198